Literacy by Design™

Assessment Guide
Theme Progress Tests and Test Practice

Rigby®
A Harcourt Achieve Imprint

www.Rigby.com
1-800-531-5015

Contents

Ongoing Test Practice

Ongoing Test Practice provides students with reading passages and questions to practice the current theme's skills. Each test includes one extended response question.

- Give the Ongoing Test Practice as homework after Lesson 7 of each theme.
- Make a transparency of the passage and questions to do more in-depth standardized test practice during class.
- Use the Answer Key on page 179 of this book to score the Ongoing Test Practice.

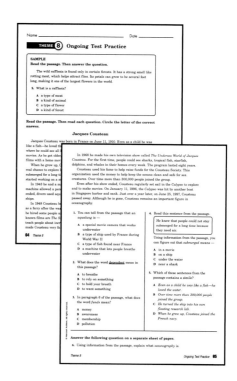

Theme Progress Tests

Theme Progress Tests cover skills and content from the student materials for each theme: comprehension, target skills, vocabulary, word study, writing, and grammar.

- Administer the Theme Progress Test on the last day of each theme.
- Two optional extended response questions may be administered with each theme.
- Extended response questions are open-book, allowing students to find text evidence to support their answers.
- Use the Student Test Record to determine students' scores using the answer key provided. Use reteaching suggestions provided for each skill if students score below the criterion score.

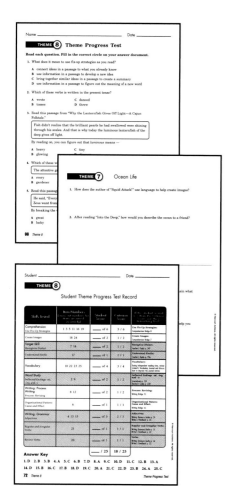

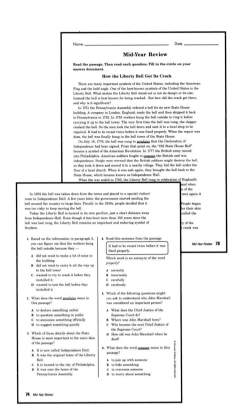

Mid-Year and End-of-Year Reviews

The Mid-Year and End-of-Year Reviews provide cumulative assessments. Students practice taking tests using new reading passages.

- The Mid-Year and End-of-Year Reviews include both extended response questions and essay prompts.
- The Student Test Record at the end of each test allows for easy scoring and provides reteaching suggestions.

Additional Resources

Test-Taking Tips and Strategies

- Pages vii and viii are blackline masters of tips and strategies students can use when taking tests.

Answer Documents

- Answer documents for Theme Progress Tests as well as Mid-Year and End-of-Year Reviews appear on pages 181 and 182 of this book.
- Copy answer documents and distribute to students at test time.
- Use a hole-punch to create a master key for each test. Place the key over each student's test to facilitate scoring.

Writing Checklist and a Lined Form for Essay Writing

- A Writing Checklist and a lined form for writing appear on pages 183 and 184 of this book.
- Distribute the Writing Checklist to students to help them write stronger essays.
- Use the lined form when administering the writing prompts found on the Mid-Year and End-of-Year Reviews.

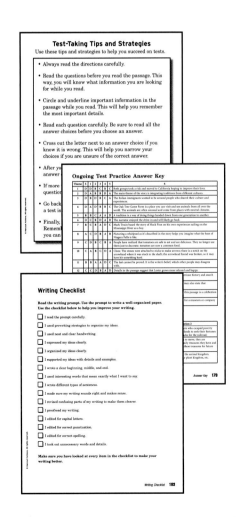

Using Rigby READS for Reading Level Placement

Ease of Student Placement

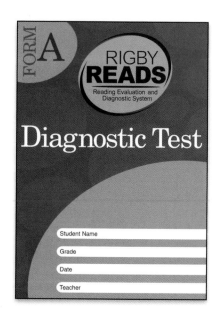

The Rigby READS (Reading Evaluation and Diagnostic System) is a valid and reliable assessment that can be administered to the whole class in a single day. On the basis of this quick and easy assessment, teachers receive the following information.

- **Placement** Each student's individual reading level for initial instruction

- **Diagnostic** A five-pillar diagnostic that pinpoints strengths and development areas in comprehension, phonics, phonemic awareness, fluency, and vocabulary

This invaluable resource is built right into the *Literacy by Design* program. Forms A and B allow you to determine end-of-year progress. The chart below shows how the Rigby READS reading levels correlate to the *Literacy by Design* reading levels.

Rigby READS Reading Level Correlation

Rigby READS Reading Level	Literacy by Design Reading Level	Rigby READS Reading Level	Literacy by Design Reading Level
Early Readiness	A	2.4	M
Kindergarten	B	3.1	N
1.1	C	3.2	O
1.2	D	3.3	P
1.3	E	4.1	Q
1.4	F	4.2	R
1.5	G	4.3	S
1.6	H	5.1	T
1.7	I	5.2	U
2.1	J	5.2	V
2.2	K	6.1	W
2.3	L		

Test-Taking Tips and Strategies

Use these tips and strategies to help you succeed on tests.

- Always read the directions carefully.

- Read the questions before you read the passage. This way, you will know what information you are looking for while you read.

- Circle and underline important information in the passage while you read. This will help you remember the most important details.

- Read each question carefully. Be sure to read all the answer choices before you choose an answer.

- Cross out the letter next to an answer choice if you know it is wrong. This will help you narrow your choices if you are unsure of the correct answer.

- After you choose an answer, reread the question and answer choice together. Do they make sense together?

- If more than one answer seems correct, read the question again. Choose the BEST answer.

- Go back and check your work if you have time. Taking a test is NOT a race to see who finishes first!

- Finally, RELAX! Taking a test can seem stressful. Remember that tests help your teacher know what you can do well and what areas you need help in.

Extended response questions ask you to write several sentences or a paragraph about a text. Use these tips to help you answer an extended response question.

- Read each question carefully.

- Use your book to review the text that the question asks about.

- Make notes before you write your answer.

- Find details and examples in the text to support your answer.

- Write your answer neatly and clearly.

- Review what you wrote. Make sure it answers the question.

- Proofread and revise your answer.

THEME ① Ongoing Test Practice

SAMPLE
Read the passage. Then answer the question.

In the late 1890s, Wilbur and Orville Wright designed one of the first aircraft. The biplane glider weighed 50 pounds and had a 17-foot wingspan. In 1900 the Wright brothers successfully tested their glider and went on to become the first men to pilot a gas-powered airplane.

S. How have airplanes changed since the Wright brothers' 1900 glider?

   A Airplanes weigh less now than they did in 1900.
   B All airplanes today have a wingspan shorter than 17 feet.
   C Airplanes are heavier and faster now than they were in 1900.
   D The Wright brothers now design larger airplanes.

Read the passage. Then read each question. Circle the letter of the correct answer.

Patrick Henry

Many people think that during the Revolutionary War, everyone living in the 13 colonies wanted to split from Great Britain. That was not the case. In fact, a lot of people were happy with the way things were. Many other people were not happy with the king, but they did not think it was worth going to war over. It took a lot of convincing to get people to change their minds and support the fight for independence. One of the loudest voices in favor of freedom came from a man named Patrick Henry.

Patrick Henry was born in Virginia in 1736. He was educated at home as a child and later studied law. He became a lawyer in 1760. Within a few years, Patrick Henry became well-known as a public speaker. When he spoke, his sincerity made people believe in what he said.

In 1765 Patrick Henry was elected to Virginia's House of Burgesses, which was the law making body of the colony of Virginia. Later that year, he gave a speech in which he spoke out against British control of Virginia. He did not think it was fair that the British king was taking the colonists' money. Patrick Henry felt that the money belonged to the colonists and their own government. It was one of the first and most memorable public outcries against the king.

Ten years later, on March 23, 1775, Patrick Henry gave his most famous speech. He was trying to convince the House of Burgesses to use its <u>military</u> to fight off the British soldiers who were starting to come into the colony. The speech was not going well, and he thought that the people listening would vote against him. Patrick Henry poured his heart into his words. At the end of his speech, he said, "Is life so dear, or peace so sweet as to be purchased at the price of chains and slavery? I know not what course others may take. But as for me, give me liberty or give me death!"

Patrick Henry's words had a powerful effect. The people stood up and shouted, "To arms! To arms!" Soon Virginia's soldiers joined with the armies of the other colonies to defend the new nation of the United States in the Revolutionary War.

1. In what way was Patrick Henry most like a salesperson?

   A He helped people decide what they should buy.
   B He worked at a store.
   C His job involved selling products to people.
   D He used words to convince people he was right.

2. In what way is the House of Burgesses like the U.S. Congress?

   A Both decide what the laws will be.
   B Both are controlled by the British king.
   C Both allow only people from Virginia to become members.
   D Both support giving money to the British king.

3. What does the word <u>military</u> mean in this passage?

   A lawmakers
   B armed forces
   C British people
   D voters

4. How has education changed since Patrick Henry was a child?

   A Most children today are educated at home.
   B Most children today are educated in a school.
   C Most children today do not get an education.
   D Most children today are educated for only a few years.

5. In what way are Americans today like the colonists before the Revolutionary War?

   A Americans today often disagree on important issues.
   B Americans today think the United States should have a king.
   C Americans today think Great Britain should be part of the United States.
   D Americans today think the United States should be part of Great Britain.

Answer the following question on a separate sheet of paper.

6. In what way was Patrick Henry's speech in 1765 like his speech in 1775?

THEME ① Theme Progress Test

Read each question. Fill in the correct circle on your answer document.

1. Which list contains only words that have short vowel sounds?

   A stroke, leaves, place
   B column, budget, closet
   C loaves, bread, butter
   D nucleus, microscope, zoom

2. What does the word <u>conflict</u> mean in the sentence below?

   > The teacher said that if the two students could not quietly settle their <u>conflict</u>, she would send them to the principal's office.

   A agreement
   B mistake
   C argument
   D friendship

3. The first step in writing an essay is —

   A proofreading   **C** revising
   B editing   **D** prewriting

4. When you make connections as you read, you —

   A relate new ideas in the text to what you already know
   B ask questions that will help you figure out the meaning of the text
   C think about ways to determine the meaning of a new word
   D determine which information in the text is most important

5. What does the word <u>defeat</u> mean in the sentence below?

   > The hometown basketball team hopes to <u>defeat</u> its rivals and move on to the playoffs.

   A play well with
   B suffer a loss to
   C win a victory over
   D practice hard for

6. Read this passage from "On Boston's Freedom Trail."

> I thought about *Johnny Tremain* when we visited Paul Revere's house. In the book, Johnny's friend Rab died at the Battle of Lexington. Paul Revere risked his life to warn others that the British were headed toward Lexington and Concord. That took courage.

What connection can you make between Rab and Paul Revere?

A Both men died in the Battle of Lexington.

B Both men played a role in the Battle of Lexington.

C Both men risked their lives to warn others.

D Both men were friends of Johnny Tremain.

7. In which of the following groups do the words all have the same initial consonant?

A memory, mission, muffle

B agree, decide, language

C giggle, hitch, silence

D command, rummage, common

8. Read this passage from "Women of the Revolution."

> In the 1700s, girls generally learned to cook, sew, and read. Young women married, raised children, and listened to their husbands. Most husbands were in charge of the money and made important decisions. By law, women could not vote or join the army. Most women did not go to school. Yet, as the thirteen colonies fought for freedom from Great Britain, women played important roles.

How are women today like women in the 1700s?

A They are not allowed to vote.

B They are not allowed to join the army.

C They fight for freedom from Great Britain.

D They make significant contributions to the United States.

9. Which of the following words has a short *a* vowel sound?

A basin

B stake

C patch

D daily

10. Read this passage from "The Nighttime Ride of Sybil Ludington."

> You've probably heard of Paul Revere. You may know Revere raced through the night to warn the Americans that the British were coming. But have you heard of Sybil Ludington? Sybil was a 16-year-old girl who went on her own nighttime ride. On April 26, 1777, British soldiers attacked a town in Connecticut. The men who made up the local American army were spread out across the countryside. Someone had to warn them. Sybil knew she was just the girl for the job!

In what way was Sybil Ludington like Paul Revere?

A Both warned people of danger.

B Both were born in Connecticut.

C Both made important rides at noon.

D Both were British soldiers.

11. What does the word <u>representatives</u> mean in this sentence?

> Our <u>representatives</u> in the U.S. Senate are called senators.

A people who live in Washington, D.C.

B people who work to overthrow the government

C people who give the views of other people who aren't present

D people who fight for freedom

12. Read these lines from "On Boston's Freedom Trail."

> We followed the Freedom Trail on a pleasant fall day. The guidebooks start the tour at the Boston Commons. We started at the end of the trail and worked our way to the start. I stopped at the Bunker Hill Monument, which stands on the site of the first major battle of the American Revolution. I could almost smell the musket fire and hear the troops in battle as I read about the fighting.

In what way is the Freedom Trail like a nature trail?

A You follow both to see famous historic places.

B Both can be found only in Boston.

C You follow both to see insects, birds, and plants.

D Both lead you along a type of path.

13. Which list contains words that all have the same initial consonant?

   A muscles, tables, chickens
   B round, rubbing, realize
   C little, rattle, brittle
   D under, unique, upside

14. Read these lines from "Women of the Revolution."

> Mary Katherine Goddard ran a newspaper, the *Maryland Journal*. Goddard did everything. She gathered the news, wrote the stories, and ran the printing press. Goddard was also a printer. She printed the first copy of the Declaration of Independence that included the names of the signers.

What connection can you make between the *Maryland Journal* and modern newspapers?

   A Both contain stories about what is happening in the world.
   B Both are written and produced by one person.
   C Both include a copy of the Declaration of Independence.
   D Both have a staff of people who work together to create the newspaper.

15. Which of the following words has a short *i* sound?

   A mighty
   B climber
   C finished
   D blinds

16. When publishing your essay, you should —

   A think about how to organize your ideas
   B read your draft to make sure your meaning is clear
   C check your writing for spelling and punctuation errors
   D share your writing with an audience

17. Which of the following is an example of a simple sentence?

   A I walk to school, but my brother drives.
   B Luis loves to run, bike, and swim.
   C He is not the fastest runner, but he works hard.
   D Luis runs long distances, and he hopes to one day compete in the Olympics.

18. Read this passage from "The Nighttime Ride of Sybil Ludington."

> SYBIL: When I overheard Father talking to the messenger from Danbury, I knew I could help. I begged him to let me go, and he finally agreed, after making me promise I would be cautious. We saddled Star, and I rode as fast as I could. I didn't want to waste time getting on and off my horse to deliver the message, so I used a long stick to bang on the doors. I yelled over the thunder and rain, "The British are burning Danbury! Gather at the Ludingtons'!"

During her ride, Sybil's stick was used mostly like —

A a doorbell   **C** a flashlight

B an automobile   **D** an umbrella

19. Read these lines from the poem "March of the Redcoats."

> Meanwhile, the riders' news was told
> With advising drums and alarming tales
> One minute . . . two . . . More and more minutemen
> Assemble for roll at Lexington.

In what way are the riders like a siren?

A Both are accompanied by a flashing light.

B Both are accompanied by drums.

C Both tell people to prepare for battle.

D Both warn people of possible danger.

Choose the word that best completes each sentence for questions 20 and 21.

20. When people overthrow a government to replace it with another government, it is called a _____.

     A military

     B union

     C revolution

     D conquer

21. When people get together, they _____.

     A assemble

     B defeat

     C conquer

     D conflict

Read this passage from "Women of the Revolution." Answer questions 22 and 23.

> Penelope Barker held a very special tea party in 1774. It was not your usual tea party. The guest list was long—51 women! Barker didn't serve British tea at her party. Instead, she served a blend of raspberry leaves and mulberry plants. Barker urged her guests to stop buying British tea and cloth. Barker thought the British <u>taxes</u> on these goods were unfair. Barker was very convincing. Most of her guests signed a pledge saying they would not buy British goods.

22. Which of the following details best supports the main idea of this passage?

   A Penelope Barker lived in Edenton, North Carolina.
   B Penelope Barker was the richest woman in North Carolina.
   C Penelope Barker died in 1796.
   D Women across the colonies followed Barker's lead and joined the boycott of British goods.

23. What does the word <u>taxes</u> mean in this passage?

   A types of tea that grow only in Great Britain
   B money paid by people to support the government
   C crackers that people eat when they drink tea
   D large groups of people who get together to talk

Read this passage. The sentences are numbered. Answer questions 24 and 25.

> (1) Tucker and Darnell are trying out for the school's football team. (2) Both hope to be the starting quarterback. (3) The starting quarterback leads the team on the field. (4) He makes important decisions about what the players will do as they play. (5) It's a difficult job, but both boys believe they can do it.

24. Which sentence is a compound sentence?

   A sentence 1   **C** sentence 4
   B sentence 2   **D** sentence 5

25. What is the subject of sentence 3?

   A field   **C** quarterback
   B team   **D** leads

Student _____ Date _____

Student Theme Progress Test Record

Skills Tested	Item Numbers (cross out numbers for items answered incorrectly)	Student Score	Criterion Score	If the student scored less than the Criterion Score, use these Reteaching Tools:
Comprehension Make Connections	4 6 8 10 12 14 18 19	_____ of 8	6 / 8	**Make Connections:** Comprehension Bridge 1
Vocabulary	2 5 11 20 21 23	_____ of 6	4 / 6	**Vocabulary:** During independent reading time, review student's Vocabulary Journal and discuss how to improve the journal entries
Word Study Short Vowels Review	1 9 15	_____ of 3	2 / 3	**Short Vowels Review:** Sourcebook p. 15 Teacher's Guide p. 8
Initial Consonants Review	7 13	_____ of 2	2 / 2	**Initial Consonants Review:** Sourcebook p. 27 Teacher's Guide p. 24
Writing: Process Writing Process: Writing Process Introduction	3 16	_____ of 2	1 / 2	**Process: Writing Process Introduction:** Writing Bridge 1
Organizational Pattern: Main Idea and Details	22	_____ of 1	1 / 1	**Organizational Pattern: Main Idea and Details:** Writing Bridge 2
Writing: Grammar Simple and Compound Sentences	17 24	_____ of 2	1 / 2	**Simple and Compound Sentences:** Writing Resource Guide p. 1 Writer's Handbook p. 35
Simple and Compound Subjects and Predicates	25	_____ of 1	1 / 1	**Simple and Compound Subjects and Predicates:** Writing Resource Guide p. 2 Writer's Handbook p. 34
		_____ / 25	18 / 25	

Answer Key

1. B 2. C 3. D 4. A 5. C 6. B 7. A 8. D 9. C 10. A 11. C 12. D 13. B

14. A 15. C 16. D 17. B 18. A 19. D 20. C 21. A 22. D 23. B 24. D 25. C

THEME ② Ongoing Test Practice

SAMPLE
Read the passage. Then answer the question.

Have you ever noticed that you cry when you cut an onion? This is because the oil that gives the onion its strong smell also irritates your eyes. When this happens, your eyes produce tears that clean your eyes and make it look like you are crying.

S. One reason your eyes produce tears is to —

    A stop you from cutting onions
    B wash away things that do not belong in your eyes
    C make it easier for you to smell strong odors
    D keep the skin on your face moist and clean

Read the passage. Then read each question. Circle the letter of the correct answer.

Park's Project

Park sat at a table in the library, looking through a big pile of books. The librarian, Mrs. Harper, noticed that he had been there for a long time and that he looked frustrated. Then Park crossed his arms and let his head fall into them with a quiet thud. Mrs. Harper walked over and asked, "Is there anything I can do to help you?"

"I have to write a paper about an important person from the Revolutionary War, but I'm not sure who to write about," Park answered. "At first I thought I'd write about Crispus Attucks."

"Who is that?" Mrs. Harper asked.

"He was a man of African American and Native American descent who lived in the late 1700s," Park explained. "He led the charge against the British soldiers at a coffee house in Boston. He and a few others died in the fighting. Before long, people started calling it the Boston Massacre."

"He sounds like an interesting person to write about," Mrs. Harper said.

"I thought so, too," Park said, "but then I thought I might write about John Paul Jones. He was the leader of the American navy during the Revolutionary War. In one battle, his ship was badly damaged and it started to sink. It looked like all was lost, but then he stood up and shouted, 'I have not yet begun to fight!' The sailors rallied and even managed to take control of the British boat."

"My favorite person from the American Revolution has always been Thomas Paine," said Mrs. Harper.

"Who's that?" Park asked.

"Thomas Paine was a writer," she replied. "Before the Revolutionary War started, there was a lot of controversy over whether the colonies should be free from Great Britain. Thomas Paine wrote a pamphlet called *Common Sense*, which explained why it no longer made sense for the colonies to be ruled by the British king. It changed a lot of people's minds. A few months later, he wrote another pamphlet called *The Crisis*. It gave people the <u>confidence</u> to fight for freedom."

"Wow," Park responded. "I didn't know that. I've made up my mind. I'm going to write about Thomas Paine."

1. Thomas Paine's pamphlet *Common Sense* was probably —

   A   very popular
   B   quickly forgotten
   C   hard to read
   D   very expensive

2. Read this sentence from the passage.

   > Then Park crossed his arms and let his head fall into them with a quiet thud.

   Which word from the sentence sounds most like the thing it describes?

   A   *crossed*   C   *thud*
   B   *head*   D   *quiet*

3. What does the word <u>confidence</u> mean in this passage?

   A   a feeling of weakness
   B   a firm belief in something
   C   a printed booklet
   D   a sense of doubt

4. The sailors in the American navy most likely found the strength to keep fighting as their boat sank because they —

   A   were inspired by the words of John Paul Jones
   B   thought the British navy would treat them well
   C   were afraid they would lose their jobs if they gave up
   D   wanted to be famous war heroes

5. In the first paragraph, Park is most likely —

   A   thinking of ways to get out of writing his report
   B   looking up information about the life of Thomas Paine
   C   trying to figure out the best way to end his essay
   D   having trouble deciding what to write about

Answer the following question on a separate sheet of paper.

6. Why does Park decide to write a report about Thomas Paine?

THEME ② Theme Progress Test

Read each question. Fill in the correct circle on your answer document.

1. Which of these words has the same consonant blend as the word *sneezed*?

   A sharing   **C** breezy

   B pleased   **D** snare

2. When you make an inference, you —

   A look for connections between two different texts you have read

   B use your own knowledge to figure out something that is not stated in the text

   C use information in the text to create images in your mind

   D look for clues in the text that will help you figure out the meaning of a word

3. When writing an essay, you should always —

   A use the same sentence structure for all your sentences

   B write sentences that are not connected to one another

   C organize your ideas in a logical way

   D write from two or more points of view

4. Which of the following should you always include when writing a story?

   A a problem and a solution

   B characters who are real people

   C an explanation of how to do something

   D your opinion about a topic

5. Read these lines from the poem "Independence Day."

   > The afternoon gets warmer, and our picnic treats are packed in ice.
   > My gladness needs no explanation—
   > It's hot outside—I love vacation!
   > I love the lazy buzzing flies.

   Which word from this passage sounds most like what it describes?

   A *warmer*

   B *lazy*

   C *outside*

   D *buzzing*

6. Which of these words has the same consonant blend as the word *colonist*?

    A traveler

    B laundry

    C east

    D color

7. Read this passage from "Gram's Declaration of Independence."

> I loved her old house with its snug nooks and crannies, and especially its musty, old attic. But Gram was busy housecleaning, getting the place ready for sale. Gram said she wanted to sell because the upkeep of the house was too time-consuming.
>
> I was in the attic sorting old papers for Gram. One by one, I went through stacks of storage boxes, throwing good stuff in one pile and junk in another.

Based on the information in this passage, you can tell that —

    A the speaker hopes that Gram will move soon

    B Gram has lived in the house for a long time

    C the speaker does not want to help Gram

    D Gram's attic smells clean and fresh

8. Which of these lists contains words that are all from the same word family?

    A tug, slug, rug

    B brittle, rattle, mitten

    C see, stare, sense

    D trip, truck, trade

9. How does an illustrator help a writer tell a story?

    A The illustrator checks the text for punctuation errors.

    B The illustrator decides what the plot of the story will be.

    C The illustrator helps express important ideas to the reader.

    D The illustrator provides the ending for the story.

10. Which of the following should you always include when writing a story?

    A historical facts

    B opinions

    C a diagram

    D a setting

11. Which of these words has the same consonant blend as *typist*?

A typical   **C** class

B priest   **D** tornado

12. Which of these words is in the same word family as *trot*?

A spot   **C** otter

B train   **D** trouble

13. Read this passage from "The Declaration of Independence."

> I joined this Second Continental Congress in June 1775. One of my tasks was to help prepare a paper. The paper outlined reasons for taking up arms against the British. Some thought my views too strong. The Congress wanted to move against the king with care. The final paper contained few of my views.

Why did the final paper contain only a few of the writer's views?

A He changed his mind and took many of his ideas out of the paper.

B Someone crossed many of his paragraphs out of the paper.

C The king told him to change the words that had been written.

D The paper was meant to represent the views of the whole group.

Read this passage from "A Statue Comes Down." Answer questions 14 and 15.

> On the way to Bowling Green, I listened as the barrel maker and the silversmith talked about what was sure to come. The king would not give up easily. There would be more fighting, perhaps even in our own city. The barrel maker asked the silversmith whether he would fight. "If I am called to stand up for America, I will gladly lend my support," he said.

14. In what way are the silversmith and the barrel maker alike?

A They are both too busy with work to go to Bowling Green.

B They both think that America is wrong and the king is right.

C They both make a living by selling things made of metal.

D They both believe that there is going to be fighting.

15. Based on the information in this passage, you can infer that the silversmith —

A strongly supports the king

B is willing to risk his life for freedom

C wants to prevent a fight from breaking out

D hopes to sell a lot of silver pots to the people in the park

Read this passage from "Gram's Declaration of Independence." Answer questions 16 and 17.

> "Perhaps we should have [the paper] appraised," Dad suggested. "This legend in the corner, 'W. J. Stone SC Washn.' might mean something important."
>
> The original <u>Declaration</u> was valuable. So, in 1820, the government asked that 200 copies be made. The printer later made some unofficial copies. The unofficial copies had the same legend as Gram's copy.

16. What does the word <u>declaration</u> mean in this passage?

    A an official statement

    B something that is old

    C a copy of a paper

    D something that is very valuable

17. Based on the legend in the corner of Gram's paper, you can tell that —

    A Gram's copy is as valuable as the original

    B Gram's copy is an original

    C Gram's copy is unofficial

    D Gram's copy belongs to the government

Read these lines from the poem "Independence Day." Answer questions 18 and 19.

> As darkness falls, the rockets rise with hissing whistles to the sky.
> We strain to find the elevation
> Of the missile's high location,
> When, with a BLAST, flames fill our eyes.

18. Which of the following words from the poem sounds most like what it describes?

    A *falls*

    B *elevation*

    C *high*

    D *hissing*

19. What are the people in this poem doing?

    A looking for a rocket in outer space

    B watching a fireworks display

    C climbing a very tall mountain

    D sitting around a campfire

Choose the word that best completes each sentence for questions 20 and 21.

20. A meeting called for a specific purpose is a _____.

   A convention

   B confidence

   C nation

   D version

21. A country that is not ruled by another country is considered _____.

   A allegiance

   B confidence

   C patriotism

   D independent

Read this passage. The sentences are numbered. Answer questions 22 and 23.

> (1) Next month the children in our class _____ going on a field trip.
> (2) Our teacher gave us a list of places and said we could choose where to go.
> (3) Some students want to go to the state museum. (4) A lot of us would rather go to the city zoo. (5) We will take a vote on Friday.

22. Which verb best completes sentence 1?

   A is

   B was

   C are

   D were

23. What is the best way to combine sentences 3 and 4?

   A Some students want to go to the state museum, but a lot of us would rather go to the city zoo.

   B Some students want to go to the state museum and to the city zoo.

   C Some students who want to go to the state museum would rather go to the city zoo.

   D Some students want to go to the state museum a lot of us would rather go to the city zoo.

Read this passage from "The Declaration of Independence." Answer questions 24 and 25.

I was sitting by Dr. Franklin. He observed that I was squirming a little with the changes to my work. I suppose I was. I believe that you can know the thoughts and feelings of a person not only by what they accept, but also by what they reject.

The debates closed on the evening of July 4th. Congress agreed to the wording. All but one member present signed the <u>document</u>. Someone then copied the words onto parchment. The delegates signed this copy on the 2nd of August.

24. What does the word <u>document</u> mean in this passage?

A a meeting where people decide what to do

B a type of pen used to sign a person's name

C a paper that contains written information

D a person who signs his or her name on something

25. How does the speaker feel during the debate?

A excited

B uneasy

C disinterested

D angry

Student _____ Date _____

THEME 2

Student Theme Progress Test Record

Skills Tested	Item Numbers (cross out numbers for items answered incorrectly)	Student Score	Criterion Score	If the student scored less than the Criterion Score, use these Reteaching Tools:
Comprehension Infer	2 7 13 15 19 25	____ of 6	5 / 6	**Infer:** Comprehension Bridge 2
Make Connections	14 17	____ of 2	1 / 2	**Make Connections:** Comprehension Bridge 1
Target Skill Understand Role of Author and Illustrator	9	____ of 1	1 / 1	**Understand Role of Author and Illustrator:** Teacher's Guide p. 49
Recognize Onomatopoeia	5 18	____ of 2	1 / 2	**Recognize Onomatopoeia:** Teacher's Guide p. 58
Vocabulary	16 20 21 24	____ of 4	3 / 4	**Vocabulary:** During independent reading time, review student's Vocabulary Journal and discuss how to improve the journal entries
Word Study Consonant Blends *sn-* and *-st*	1 6 11	____ of 3	2 / 3	**Consonant Blends *sn-* and *-st*:** Sourcebook p. 45 Teacher's Guide p. 40
Word Families	8 12	____ of 2	1 / 2	**Word Families:** Sourcebook p. 57 Teacher's Guide p. 56
Writing: **Process Writing** Trait: Traits Introduction	3	____ of 1	1 / 1	**Trait: Traits Introduction:** Writing Bridge 3
Form: Story	4 10	____ of 2	1 / 2	**Form: Story:** Writing Bridge 4
Writing: Grammar Subject-Verb Agreement	22	____ of 1	1 / 1	**Subject-Verb Agreement:** Writing Resource Guide p. 3 Writer's Handbook p. 24
Sentence Combining	23	____ of 1	1 / 1	**Sentence Combining:** Writing Resource Guide p. 4 Writer's Handbook p. 45
		/ 25	**18 / 25**	

Answer Key

1. D   2. B   3. C   4. A   5. D   6. C   7. B   8. A   9. C   10. D   11. B   12. A   13. D

14. D   15. B   16. A   17. C   18. D   19. B   20. A   21. D   22. C   23. A   24. C   25. B

THEME ③ Ongoing Test Practice

SAMPLE
Read the passage. Then answer the question.

In 1873 two men in the Old West came up with a new kind of pants. The pants were made of a blue cloth called denim, and they had pockets with rivets. Many cowboys, miners, and other workers bought the pants. Today we call these pants blue jeans.

S. Which question might you ask to help you figure out why cowboys and miners liked the new pants?

  A How many pairs of denim pants did the two men sell?
  B What are the names of the men who invented the pants?
  C Why were the new pants made of blue cloth?
  D What was special about pants that had rivets in the pockets?

Read the passage. Then read each question. Circle the letter of the correct answer.

John Hancock

When you look closely at the Declaration of Independence, you see a big group of names at the bottom. These are the names of the men who signed it, promising that the 13 colonies would stand together as a new, free country called the United States of America. Of all these signatures, one name stands out most. John Hancock's signature is in the center of the page at the top of all the other names. It is also the largest name on the page.

John Hancock was an important figure in the Revolutionary War and in the formation of the United States. As the leader of the Second Continental Congress, he named George Washington the leader of the whole American army. When the Declaration was presented to the group on July 4, 1776, Hancock was the only person to sign it. The other 55 people signed their names on August 22, 1776.

A story soon grew about Hancock. People said that he wrote his name large and neatly so King George the Third would be able to read it without his glasses. While this is an interesting story, most historians now believe that Hancock always signed his name this way.

Hancock's most important job during the war was getting money and supplies so Americans would have what they needed to win the war. When the war ended,

Hancock helped organize the new government. He served as the seventh president of the United States in Congress before the position of president of the United States was created. He also helped establish an official navy for the country and served as governor of Massachusetts.

Today many things are named after John Hancock, including a town in Massachusetts, a large insurance company, a number of buildings, and several ships. And to this day, people <u>connect</u> the name "John Hancock" with a person's signature.

1. What question might you ask based on the first paragraph of the passage?

   A Who else signed the Declaration of Independence?
   B Where was John Hancock born?
   C Where is the original Declaration of Independence kept?
   D In what state was the Declaration of Independence signed?

2. Which of the following details belongs in paragraph 4?

   A In 1774 Hancock spoke out against the British.
   B Hancock died in 1793.
   C Hancock was an admired speaker.
   D Hancock worked to keep troops fed and helped them support their families.

3. What does the word <u>connect</u> mean in this passage?

   A to buy insurance
   B to write your name
   C to join things together
   D to give something a name

4. What question might you ask based on paragraph 4 of the passage?

   A Who established the army of the United States?
   B When was the position of president of the United States created?
   C Where is the governor's office in Massachusetts?
   D Who is the current president of the United States?

5. What question would you ask to better understand the last paragraph of the passage?

   A Why do people call a signature a "John Hancock"?
   B What type of insurance does the insurance company named after John Hancock sell?
   C What other towns in Massachusetts are named after people?
   D Who decided to name ships after John Hancock?

Answer the following question on a separate sheet of paper.

6. Based on information from the passage, why do you think John Hancock was the only person to sign the Declaration of Independence on July 4, 1776?

THEME ③ Theme Progress Test

Read each question. Fill in the correct circle on your answer document.

1. When you write an essay, you should —

   A force the reader to work hard to figure out the message
   B include details that support the main idea
   C discuss as many different topics as possible
   D express all your ideas in exactly the same way

2. Asking questions as you read helps you —

   A prepare to read another text
   B predict what will happen in the next text you read
   C connect ideas from a text to your own life
   D make sense of the text

3. Read this passage from "Bake Your Own Bread."

   > Dissolve the sugar in the warm water and then stir in the yeast. Because yeasts are living, one-celled fungi, make sure the water is not too hot or it will kill the yeast cells. The mixture will foam as the yeast cells make carbon dioxide and ethanol bubbles. These bubbles cause the dough to rise.

   You would most likely use yeast to —

   A help you dissolve sugar into warm water
   B make bread that is dry and flat
   C make the bread fluffy and light
   D make the bread smell good

4. What does the word <u>reassured</u> mean in the sentence below?

   > I thought my cold would last forever, but my mother <u>reassured</u> me that it would pass in a few days.

   A gave someone medicine
   B made someone feel like laughing
   C frightened someone
   D made someone feel more confident

5. Which word in the sentence below is a noun?

> I went to see my doctor yesterday for a yearly physical exam.

A *my*

B *doctor*

C *yesterday*

D *for*

6. Read this passage from "The Heat Is On!"

> **SOLAR OVEN** The Sun's . . . energy reflects on the surface of the oven and transfers heat to the food.

Which question might you ask about this passage?

A How big is the Sun?

B How hot does a solar oven get?

C How far away is the Sun?

D What kind of food is being cooked?

7. Which words in the sentence below are nouns?

> The teacher stayed up during the night correcting homework.

A stayed, during, homework

B teacher, up, during

C stayed, during, correcting

D teacher, night, homework

8. Read this passage from "Let's Get Cooking!"

> "When I first started working in a commercial bakery, we had a huge conventional oven. We could bake up to eight cake layers at once. That's enough to build two three-tiered wedding cakes."

The bakery most likely had a big oven because —

A many people bought cakes from the bakery

B the owner of the bakery could not find a smaller oven to buy

C the layers of a wedding cake must be baked at the same time

D the owner of the bakery needed to fill space in the kitchen

9. Which list contains words that are all nouns?

   A sizzle, pour, burning
   B quickly, carefully, quietly
   C curious, thoughtful, dry
   D floor, cabin, machine

10. Read this passage from "The Heat Is On!"

> **MICROWAVE OVENS** The first microwave stood nearly 6 ft tall and weighed over 750 lbs. Electromagnetic waves in a microwave heat the molecules in food.

Which of the following questions could you ask to better understand this passage?

   A What other machines use electromagnetic waves?
   B Why was the first microwave oven so large?
   C How long does it take to cook popcorn in a microwave oven?
   D What is the most popular brand of microwave oven?

11. Which list contains only words that have long vowel sounds?

   A place, home, write
   B stirred, stunned, staple
   C mantle, sample, package
   D wander, spend, walk

12. Which of the following statements is true of good writing?

   A Good writing discusses many different topics at once.
   B Good writing expresses ideas in an uninteresting way.
   C Good writing has a clear message or story.
   D Good writing lacks supporting details.

13. Which of the following words from the sentence below has a long vowel sound?

> I realized that I wrote the wrong word, so I had to erase it.

   A *wrong*
   B *that*
   C *wrote*
   D *word*

Read this passage. The sentences are numbered. Answer questions 14 and 15.

(1) Have you ever gone skiing? (2) Try it sometime. (3) My school's ski club goes to a local mountain a few times every winter. (4) Skiing is a lot of fun because you get to ride a chair lift. (5) Another reason it is fun is that you get to go really fast when you ski down the mountain. (6) I really love to ski!

14. What is the best way to combine sentences 4 and 5?

   A Two reasons that skiing is fun are the chair lift and going fast.
   B Skiing is a lot of fun because you get to ride a chair lift, another reason that it is fun is because you get to go really fast when you ski down the mountain.
   C Skiing is a lot of fun because you get to ride a chair lift, but you get to go really fast when you ski down the mountain.
   D Skiing is a lot of fun because you get to ride a chair lift and you can go really fast when you ski down the mountain.

15. Which sentence from the passage tells you to do something?

   A sentence 1
   B sentence 2
   C sentence 3
   D sentence 4

Choose the word that best completes each sentence for questions 16 and 17.

16. The smallest particles you can divide something into without changing it into something else are _____.

   A ingredients
   B radiation
   C molecules
   D chemicals

17. The process of giving off heat or energy in the form of invisible rays or waves is called _____.

   A radiation
   B scientific
   C transfer
   D convection

Read this passage from "Abuela's Feast." Answer questions 18 and 19.

> "Steaming must use <u>conduction</u> since it uses a pan, steam, and food. My science teacher would like this. We're putting scientific information to use," Gabriel smiled proudly. "Is that all the food we are going to have and all the cooking we'll be doing, Abuela?"

18. Which question could you ask to help you better understand this passage?

   A What type of food does Gabriel's science teacher like best?
   B What types of food are cooked in a pan?
   C What other food does Gabriel want to cook?
   D How is scientific information useful in cooking?

19. What does the word <u>conduction</u> mean in this passage?

   A the temperature of a pan
   B the movement of heat through materials
   C a scientific method
   D a type of pan used for steaming vegetables

Read this passage from "Let's Get Cooking!" Answer questions 20 and 21.

> Think about cooking pancakes on top of the stove in a pan. First, the pan gets hot from the burner's flame. Then the hot pan <u>transfers</u> its heat to the batter, which browns into nice pancakes. The metal pan acts as a "conductor" of heat. You have to flip the pancake to cook it on the other side. The heat comes from only one direction and travels through something solid (in this instance, the metal of the pan).

20. Which of the following questions could you ask to help you better understand this passage?

   A Who invented the modern stove?
   B What kind of syrup goes best with pancakes?
   C Where does the heat go when it hits the pancake batter?
   D Where does the speaker buy her pancake mix?

21. What does the word <u>transfers</u> mean in this passage?

   A moves from one place to another
   B places a pan on a stove
   C turns a liquid into a solid
   D uses a flame to cook something

Read this passage from "Bake Your Own Bread." Answer questions 22 and 23.

> 1. Mix the flour and water together in a large bowl. If the dough is sticking to the sides of the bowl, add more water until all the dough can be shaped into a ball.
> 2. Sprinkle some flour on the wooden cutting board. Then knead the ball for 10 minutes.
> 3. Split the ball in half.

22. Which question should you ask to help you better understand step 2?

    A How big should the ball of dough be when I take it out of the bowl?

    B What are some different types of flour that I can use?

    C Why is it important to put flour on the cutting board?

    D How long does the dough need to cook?

23. How is this passage organized?

    A most important to least important information

    B the order in which steps should occur

    C strongest argument to weakest argument

    D least important to most important information

Read this passage from "Abuela's Feast." Answer questions 24 and 25.

> "I'm going to get my camera before we start cooking," Gabriel said. "I'll take pictures of the food ready to cook, cooking, and on platters and in bowls. This project will really impress my science teacher—and make him hungry!"

24. Based on the information in this passage, you can infer that —

    A Gabriel wants to be a science teacher

    B Gabriel wants to take pictures of the food because it looks delicious

    C Gabriel is excited to taste the food

    D Gabriel wants to take pictures of the cooking process for a science project

25. What question might you ask based on this passage?

    A How will taking pictures of food improve Gabriel's project?

    B What types of food does Gabriel like best?

    C How many platters and bowls will Gabriel need?

    D What kind of camera is best for taking pictures of food?

Student _____ Date _____

THEME 3

Student Theme Progress Test Record

Skills Tested	Item Numbers (cross out numbers for items answered incorrectly)	Student Score	Criterion Score	If the student scored less than the Criterion Score, use these Reteaching Tools:
Comprehension Ask Questions	2 6 10 18 20 22 25	___ of 7	5 / 7	**Ask Questions:** Comprehension Bridge 3
Infer	3 8 24	___ of 3	2 / 3	**Infer:** Comprehension Bridge 2
Vocabulary	4 16 17 19 21	___ of 5	4 / 5	**Vocabulary:** During independent reading time, review student's Vocabulary Journal and discuss how to improve the journal entries
Word Study Long Vowels Review	11 13	___ of 2	1 / 2	**Long Vowels Review:** Sourcebook p. 77 Teacher's Guide p. 74
Writing: Process Writing Trait: Ideas	1 12	___ of 2	1 / 2	**Trait: Ideas:** Writing Bridge 5
Organizational Pattern: Sequence	23	___ of 1	1 / 1	**Organizational Pattern:** **Sequence:** Writing Bridge 6
Writing: Grammar Nouns	5 7 9	___ of 3	2 / 3	**Nouns:** Writing Resource Guide p. 11 Writer's Handbook p. 20
Review Sentence Combining	14	___ of 1	1 / 1	**Sentence Combining:** Writing Resource Guide p. 5 Writer's Handbook p. 45
Sentence Types: Declarative, Interrogative, Imperative, Exclamatory	15	___ of 1	1 / 1	**Sentence Types: Declarative,** **Interrogative, Imperative,** **Exclamatory:** Writing Resource Guide p. 6 Writer's Handbook p. 35
		/ 25	18 / 25	

Answer Key

1. B 2. D 3. C 4. D 5. B 6. B 7. D 8. A 9. D 10. B 11. A 12. C 13. C

14. D 15. B 16. C 17. A 18. D 19. B 20. C 21. A 22. C 23. B 24. D 25. A

THEME ④ Ongoing Test Practice

SAMPLE
Read the passage. Then answer the question.

February is my favorite month. I love Valentine's Day, which falls on February 14. Presidents' Day is celebrated on the third Monday of the month. Best of all, my birthday is February 27.

S. What is the most important sentence in this passage?

A *February is my favorite month.*
B *I love Valentine's Day, which falls on February 14.*
C *Presidents' Day is celebrated on the third Monday of the month.*
D *Best of all, my birthday is February 27.*

Read the passage. Then read each question. Circle the letter of the correct answer.

The Recipe Contest

"Are they ready yet?" John asked.

"Yes, but we need to let them cool for a little while," Aunt Margaret answered.

"I can't wait," Annie added. "You make the best chocolate chip cookies ever!"

"You know, I saw an ad for a recipe contest in a magazine the other day," John said. "You should enter. First prize is five hundred dollars!"

Aunt Margaret thought it over for a moment and then said, "Why not?" She spent a few days adjusting her cookie recipe, adding and removing ingredients. When she decided that she had the perfect formula, she wrote it down and mailed it in to the magazine.

"They're going to print the winner's name in the next issue of the magazine," Aunt Margaret told the children. "It comes out in a few weeks."

Even though it was a relatively short <u>length</u> of time to wait, those few weeks seemed to drag on forever. Aunt Margaret found herself checking the calendar several times a day. She tried to find ways to keep busy. She did a lot of work around the house, but she couldn't stop thinking about the contest.

Then a few days before the magazine was due on the newsstands, Aunt Margaret got a call. John and Annie were nearby and listened to her conversation.

"Yes, I submitted the chocolate chip cookie recipe," she said to the mysterious

caller. "I see. Well, that is good news. Thank you so much for calling! Goodbye."
With that, she hung up the phone.

"You won!" Annie shouted with glee before Aunt Margaret could say a word.

"No," Aunt Margaret replied. "A woman from Toledo, Ohio, won for a banana bread recipe she sent in."

"So who called you?" John asked with a puzzled look. "I thought you said it was good news."

"It was," Aunt Margaret replied, as happy as a lark. "The call came from the owner of the Culinary Cookie Company. I didn't win the contest, but he liked my cookies so much that he offered to buy my recipe for $1,000!"

"I'd say you won after all!" Annie exclaimed.

1. Which source would you use to find out where Toledo, Ohio, is?

   A   a dictionary
   B   an almanac
   C   a thesaurus
   D   an atlas

2. Which of the following sentences from the story best shows alliteration?

   A   *Annie shouted with glee before Aunt Margaret could say a word.*
   B   *She tried to find ways to keep busy.*
   C   *"It was," Aunt Margaret replied, as happy as a lark.*
   D   *"The call came from the owner of the Culinary Cookie Company."*

3. What does the word <u>length</u> mean in this passage?

   A   how important something is
   B   how slowly something happens
   C   how long something is
   D   how patient someone is

4. Which of these details from the story is most important?

   A   Margaret is John and Annie's aunt.
   B   Aunt Margaret submitted a recipe for a contest.
   C   John and Annie love Aunt Margaret's cookies.
   D   The cookies had to cool before anyone could eat them.

5. Which of these details is least important to the main idea of the story?

   A   Aunt Margaret did a lot of work around the house.
   B   Aunt Margaret adjusted her cookie recipe until she thought she had the perfect formula.
   C   Aunt Margaret submitted a chocolate chip cookie recipe to a contest.
   D   The Culinary Cookie Company offered to buy Aunt Margaret's recipe for $1,000.

Answer the following question on a separate sheet of paper.

6. Why is it important in the story that Aunt Margaret did not win the contest?

THEME ④ Theme Progress Test

Read each question. Fill in the correct circle on your answer document.

1. What does it mean to determine importance as you read?

   A figure out whether people consider the text to be important
   B decide which details are most important to the main idea
   C look for sentences that mean the same thing in the passage
   D summarize the important events in a passage

2. What does the word improvise mean in the sentence below?

   > The actress forgot her lines, so she had to improvise for the rest of the scene.

   A memorize lines for a play
   B try to remember something important
   C stop what you are doing
   D make things up as you go along

3. Which words in the sentence below are proper nouns?

   > Our friend Donna asked if we would like to see a movie at the theater in Nashville on Friday night.

   A friend, movie, theater
   B Our, if, we
   C Donna, Nashville, Friday
   D asked, like, see

4. When you are writing a poem, what is the best way to appeal to the imagination of a reader?

   A use descriptive language
   B use long, difficult words
   C write from many different points of view
   D write about many different topics

5. If you wanted to learn about the French Revolution, you would look in —

   A an atlas
   B a thesaurus
   C a dictionary
   D an encyclopedia

6. Which of the following lists of words contains all proper nouns?

    A carpenter, flag, bookcase

    B Jeremy, October, Pennsylvania

    C we, they, us

    D travel, consider, juggle

7. Read this passage from "The Smell of Soup and the Sound of Money—A Tale from Turkey."

> Finally, Hodja addressed the innkeeper. "You demand payment for the smell of your soup," he said. "Is that correct?" The innkeeper shook his head eagerly in reply, "Yes, I do." Hodja then addressed the traveler. "But you have no money to pay. Is that correct?" The traveler looked sadly toward the floor and answered, "That is correct."

Which of the following details is most important in this passage?

    A Hodja talks to both the innkeeper and the traveler.

    B The traveler looks sadly toward the floor.

    C The innkeeper wants to be paid for the smell of the soup.

    D The innkeeper eagerly shakes his head in reply to Hodja.

8. What should you do first if you are writing an essay about violins?

    A write down ideas about violins

    B look for misspelled words in your essay

    C turn your ideas about violins into complete sentences

    D look for unimportant details in your essay

9. Which words in the sentences below are proper nouns?

> Frank Sinatra was a famous musician born in New Jersey. He was also an excellent actor who even won the prized Oscar award.

    A famous, excellent, prized

    B was, born, won

    C musician, actor, award

    D Frank Sinatra, New Jersey, Oscar

10. To find out where an author found the information used in a book, you would look in —

    A the bibliography   **C** an encyclopedia

    B a dictionary   **D** an almanac

11. Read this passage from "Sounds Good to Me!"

> The outer part of a person's ear collects sound waves as the waves travel through the air. These waves strike tiny bones in the middle ear and cause them to vibrate. The inner ear picks up the vibrations, and the brain recognizes them as sound. People who have difficulty hearing may benefit from a hearing aid.

Which sentence contains information that is not important to the main idea of the passage?

  A *The inner ear picks up the vibrations, and the brain recognizes them as sound.*

  B *The outer part of a person's ear collects sound waves as the waves travel through the air.*

  C *People who have difficulty hearing may benefit from a hearing aid.*

  D *These waves strike tiny bones in the middle ear and cause them to vibrate.*

Read these lines from the poem "Riding the Sound Waves." Answer questions 12 and 13.

> Rafe ripped a riff so wild and true
> It lifted my Mrs. Masters clear out of her shoes
> Whirled her 'round the gym and then
> Set her back in her shoes again.
>
> His pounding rhythm made the skeleton hop
> Off its hook and onto the table top
> It rumba'd and calypso'd and do-si-do'd
> Those bones did the two-step to a minor mode.

12. Which of these lines from the poem contains the best example of alliteration?

  A *Set her back in her shoes again*

  B *His pounding rhythm made the skeleton hop*

  C *Whirled her 'round the gym and then*

  D *Rafe ripped a riff so wild and true*

13. How do you know that this is a poem?

  A It tells a story.

  B It uses rhythm and rhyme.

  C It explains the meaning of a word.

  D It describes a real event.

Read this passage. The sentences are numbered. Answer questions 14 and 15.

(1) It was the beginning of January, and the _____ at Lincoln Elementary were playing hockey on the frozen pond. (2) They practiced hard every Friday because the annual hockey tournament was coming up. (3) Coach Henderson thought the players looked great and that the team would be tough to beat.

14. Which of the following words best completes sentence 1?

   A child

   B childs

   C childrens

   D children

15. Which of the following words from the passage are all proper nouns?

   A They, Henderson, players

   B January, Lincoln, Friday

   C playing, practiced, looked

   D pond, hockey, team

Read these lines from the poem "Riding the Sound Waves." Answer questions 16 and 17.

Uncle Rafe was my exhibit for the Science Fair
His musical <u>vibrations</u> moved much more than air.
Jazz and Blues or Rock and Pop
When he gets a place pumpin', it never stops. . . .

Uncle's music moved us all in a major way.
Yeah, my ribbon was blue at the end of the day!
You should've heard those science judges rave,
When we showed them how to ride a sound wave.

16. Which line from the poem contains the best example of alliteration?

   A *Uncle Rafe was my exhibit for the Science Fair*

   B *Jazz and Blues or Rock and Pop*

   C *Uncle's music moved us all in a major way*

   D *You should've heard those science judges rave*

17. What does the word <u>vibrations</u> mean in this poem?

   A rapid back and forth movements

   B kinds of music

   C types of sounds

   D types of guitars

Read this passage from "The Smell of Soup and the Sound of Money—A Tale from Turkey." Answer questions 18 and 19.

> One day, a woman spotted the traveler through a thick crowd, and she took pity on him. Without saying a word, she held out her hand and offered the man a piece of bread. The woman had little to give, and this was all she could spare.
>
> The woman's generosity startled the traveler. Nobody had paid attention to him like this before. When he tried to thank the woman, she turned abruptly and hurried on her way. As she disappeared into the crowd, the man began to smile. For the first time in weeks, he felt hope. He looked at his piece of bread in amazement and thought, "How nice it would be if I had something to put on this bread!"

18. What question should you ask to better understand how the woman felt when she gave the traveler bread?

    A What kind of bread did the woman give to the traveler?

    B Where was the woman going?

    C Why did the woman hurry away?

    D How did the woman spot the traveler through the thick crowd?

19. Which detail from the passage is interesting but not important?

    A The woman gave the traveler some bread.

    B There was a thick crowd.

    C The traveler was startled by the woman's generosity.

    D The bread gave the traveler a sense of hope.

Choose the word that best completes each sentence for questions 20 and 21.

20. When different tunes in a song go together well, they form a _____.

    A harmony

    B broadcast

    C pitch

    D vibration

21. A musical _____ is a device for producing sounds.

    A experiment

    B melody

    C instrument

    D broadcast

Read this passage from "Sounds Good to Me!" Answer questions 22 and 23.

> This exhibit compares the loudness of different sounds. Scientists measure loudness in decibels (dB). A busy street is louder than an average home. Sounds louder than a vacuum cleaner can cause hearing loss over time. Very loud sounds, like jet planes, can cause immediate hearing loss.

22. What is the most important idea in this passage?

   A The average home is quieter than a busy street.

   B The abbreviation for "decibels" is "dB."

   C Loudness is measured in units called decibels.

   D Very loud sounds can damage a person's hearing.

23. What question might you ask to help you avoid the risk of hearing loss?

   A Why are jet plane engines so loud?

   B What are some examples of very soft sounds?

   C How many decibels does the sound of a vacuum cleaner make?

   D What kind of education do you need to become a scientist?

Read these lines from the song "I Love a Piano." Answer questions 24 and 25.

> As a child I went wild when a band played.
> How I ran to the man when his hand swayed.
> Clarinets were my pets, and a slide trombone I thought was simply divine
> But today, when they play, I could miss them.
> Ev'ry bar is a jar to my system.
> But there's one musical instrument that I call mine . . .

24. What is the main idea of this song?

   A The narrator wants to be a member of a marching band.

   B The narrator used to like many instruments, but now he likes only one.

   C The narrator wishes he knew how to play a clarinet or a slide trombone.

   D The narrator has fond memories of musicians from his childhood.

25. How do you know that this song is told from the first-person point of view?

   A The narrator uses the words *I*, *my*, and *mine*.

   B The narrator uses rhyming words.

   C The narrator talks about music.

   D The narrator uses the words *pets*, *divine*, and *jar*.

Student _____ Date _____

THEME ④

Student Theme Progress Test Record

Skills Tested	Item Numbers (cross out numbers for items answered incorrectly)	Student Score	Criterion Score	If the student scored less than the Criterion Score, use these Reteaching Tools:
Comprehension Determine Importance	1 7 11 19 22 24	____ of 6	5 / 6	**Determine Importance:** Comprehension Bridge 4
Ask Questions	18 23	____ of 2	1 / 2	**Ask Questions:** Comprehension Bridge 3
Target Skill Recognize Alliteration	12 16	____ of 2	1 / 2	**Recognize Alliteration:** Teacher's Guide p. 115
Identify Point of View	25	____ of 1	1 / 1	**Identify Point of View:** Teacher's Guide p. 124
Vocabulary	2 17 20 21	____ of 4	3 / 4	**Vocabulary:** During independent reading time, review student's Vocabulary Journal and discuss how to improve the journal entries
Word Study Reference Materials	5 10	____ of 2	1 / 2	**Reference Materials:** Sourcebook p. 119 Teacher's Guide p. 122
Writing: Process Writing Process: Prewriting	8	____ of 1	1 / 1	**Process: Prewriting:** Writing Bridge 7
Form: Poem	4 13	____ of 2	1 / 2	**Form: Poem:** Writing Bridge 8
Writing: Grammar Common and Proper Nouns	3 6 9 15	____ of 4	3 / 4	**Common and Proper Nouns:** Writing Resource Guide p. 7 Writer's Handbook p. 20
Singular and Plural Nouns	14	____ of 1	1 / 1	**Singular and Plural Nouns:** Writing Resource Guide p. 8 Writer's Handbook p. 20
		____ / 25	18 / 25	

Answer Key

1. B   2. D   3. C   4. A   5. D   6. B   7. C   8. A   9. D   10. A   11. C   12. D   13. B

14. D   15. B   16. C   17. A   18. C   19. B   20. A   21. C   22. D   23. C   24. B   25. A

THEME ⑤ Ongoing Test Practice

SAMPLE
Read the passage. Then answer the question.

If you put your money into a savings account at a bank, you will earn money, called interest, for keeping your savings there. If you borrow money from the bank, you pay interest to the bank. The interest you pay is then given to people with savings accounts.

S. Where does a bank get the money it pays to people with savings accounts?

A from people with savings accounts
B from people who borrow money
C from people who are paid interest
D from people who lend money

Read the passage. Then read each question. Circle the letter of the correct answer.

Lana's Stuffy Head

Lana woke up one morning and noticed that her head felt like it was all stuffed up. She climbed out of bed, put on her slippers, and went downstairs. When she found her mother making breakfast, she said, "Mom, my head hurts."

"Sounds like you've got a bad head cold," her mother replied. "I'd better call Dr. Peterson."

A few hours later, Lana was sitting patiently in a little room, waiting for Dr. Peterson. Finally the door opened, and Dr. Peterson came in. "Hello, Lana," Dr. Peterson said. "I hear you're not feeling well today. Your head's all stuffed up, huh?"

Lana nodded, and Dr. Peterson took out a stethoscope to listen to Lana breathe. "Your chest sounds clear. Can you show me where your head feels the worst?"

Lana pointed to the area between her eyes. "I think you've got a sinus infection," Dr. Peterson said. "You've got extra fluid in your head. That's why it feels so full."

"Why does everything sound <u>funny</u>?" Lana asked.

"Let me explain how your ears work," Dr. Peterson said. She showed Lana a diagram of an ear and began to speak, <u>tracing</u> her finger around the parts of the ear as she spoke. "When sound travels into your ear, it causes a vibration on your eardrum, which is right inside your ear. Behind the eardrum are three very small bones in your middle ear. When the eardrum vibrates, these bones start to vibrate. Behind the middle ear is the inner ear, which is full of fluid. When the vibrations hit the fluid, they turn into special messages that go to your brain. Your brain tells you that you are hearing a sound. Because you have so much extra fluid in your head right now, the vibrations sound a little different."

"And when the extra fluid goes away, I'll hear correctly again?" Lana asked.

"You've got it!" Dr. Peterson replied.

That sounded just fine to Lana.

1. Why does Lana's mother call the doctor?

   A She wants to invite the doctor to breakfast.
   B She wants the doctor to see Lana.
   C She is not feeling well and wants to see the doctor.
   D She wants the doctor to talk to Lana on the phone.

2. What does the word <u>tracing</u> mean in this passage?

   A drawing on a page with a pencil
   B explaining how something works
   C describing how someone feels
   D following the outline of something

3. Why does Dr. Peterson show Lana a diagram of an ear?

   A to help her understand how people hear
   B to show her the best way to clean her ears
   C to explain why she should never put anything in her ear
   D to explain how loud sounds can hurt her ears

4. Read the meanings below for the word <u>funny</u>.

   > **funny**
   > **1.** causing laughter
   > **2.** unusual **3.** tricky **4.** silly

   Which meaning best fits the way <u>funny</u> is used in the passage?

   A meaning 1
   B meaning 2
   C meaning 3
   D meaning 4

5. Why does Dr. Peterson use a stethoscope on Lana?

   A She wants to listen to see if Lana's heartbeat is unusual.
   B She wants to find out why Lana's throat is sore.
   C She wants to find out if Lana is having any trouble breathing.
   D She wants to take a picture of Lana's lungs with an X-ray machine.

Answer the following question on a separate sheet of paper.

6. According to the passage, how does sound get from the ear to the brain?

THEME ⑤ Theme Progress Test

Read each question. Fill in the correct circle on your answer document.

1. Which of these words is a synonym of the word *worried*?

   A concerned

   B calm

   C outgoing

   D relaxed

2. What does the word <u>inform</u> mean in the sentence below?

   > When the lightbulb in the supply closet burned out, Tina went to <u>inform</u> the janitor so he could change it.

   A to collect supplies

   B to change a lightbulb

   C to look for someone

   D to give facts

3. Which of the following should you do when drafting an essay?

   A look for errors in spelling and capitalization

   B organize prewriting ideas into sentences

   C check that verbs agree with their subject

   D copy the final essay in very neat handwriting

4. When you monitor understanding as you read, you —

   A bring pieces of information together to form a new idea

   B think about questions you have in your mind as you read

   C stop and think about whether you understand what you have read so far

   D combine what you read and what you already know to predict what will happen next

5. Which of the following best describes a biography?

   A the story of a person's life

   B the history of an important building

   C a story about an event that really happened

   D a description of a recent event

6. Read this passage from "A Not Very Well-Kept Secret."

> At that moment Benjamin Franklin—yes, *the* Ben Franklin—hobbled into the dining room (his gout was obviously bothering him a great deal). We all wanted to melt into the floor. Mr. Franklin looked around, surveying the scene. He picked up an apple and took a bite out of it, and then used the apple to point around the room. "Who got this started?" he asked.

How do the boys feel when Ben Franklin walks into the room?

A impressed

B angry

C proud

D ashamed

7. What does the word *park* mean in the sentence below?

> As Erica tried to park her car, she drove it over the curb.

A a public playground

B to steer a car into a space

C place or settle for a long time

D a stadium for ball games

8. Which sentence contains an antonym of the word *ridiculous*?

A The clown at the circus wore a very silly outfit.

B The annoying fly kept buzzing around my head.

C Many of the students' ideas were sensible.

D Some of Mary's cautious friends decided to stay home.

9. A document that describes a proposed law is called —

A an article

B an amendment

C a preamble

D a bill

10. What does the word *book* mean in the sentence below?

> After reading the article about Bermuda, Peter decided to book a family vacation there.

A a packet of stamps or matches

B a volume of pages bound together

C to make a reservation

D to leave a place quickly

11. Which of the following words is a synonym of the word *league*?

A group

B large

C strong

D individual

12. Read this passage from "James Madison: Father of the Constitution."

> James Madison was born in Virginia in 1751. His parents owned a plantation near the Blue Ridge Mountains. Young James loved books and learning. At 18, he left home for college in New Jersey. There he learned new ideas about government. Madison left college firmly believing that good government and freedom go hand in hand. He was also sure that a good government requires a balance of power. These views would play important roles in the future of the United States.

Which of these details from this passage is most important?

A James Madison believed good government was important for freedom.

B James Madison lived in Virginia as a boy and then moved to New Jersey.

C James Madison left home and went to college when he was 18 years old.

D James Madison's parents owned a plantation near the Blue Ridge Mountains.

13. Read these lines from the poem "The Bill of Rights."

> I'm a part of *we the people*,
> A *we* that's made of individuals,
> Individuals who can take shelter
> Under certain basic rights
> Just to read a paper
> Or watch the evening news

When the narrator says that she is a part of *we the people,* she means that she —

A is from a large family

B is a citizen of the United States

C is an individual

D is a member of a club

14. During the drafting stage of writing, you should concentrate on —

A deciding on a topic to write about

B correcting spelling mistakes

C turning ideas into sentences

D correcting punctuation errors

15. Read this passage from "Harriet Tubman Leads the Way."

> But something secret was going on. It was called the Underground Railroad. The Underground Railroad wasn't under the ground. And it wasn't a railroad. It was a network of people who helped escaped slaves make their way to freedom in the North. The network included "conductors" and "station masters." Conductors acted as guides. Station masters provided safe houses. Both risked their own safety to help others escape from slavery.

Which information about the Underground Railroad is most important?

A The Underground Railroad wasn't located underground.

B The Underground Railroad included conductors and station masters.

C The Underground Railroad helped slaves escape to freedom.

D The Underground Railroad wasn't a real railroad.

Read this passage from "A Not Very Well-Kept Secret." Answer questions 16 and 17.

> Of course, we each thought of the man whose room we tended as "our" delegate. And we took everything we heard that person say to heart. If I overheard George Mason say the [document] was flawed, I agreed with him. If he said each person's rights should be spelled out, I was ready to fight for that idea. Tom said the federal government should be strong. Why? Because that is what Mr. Hamilton thought.

16. As used in this passage, the word *rights* means —

A things that are correct

B privileges that belong to people

C truth and justice

D claims to property

17. Why did Tom say that the federal government should be strong?

A He thought that each person's rights should be spelled out.

B He believed that Mr. Hamilton had the wrong idea.

C He felt that George Mason had the best ideas.

D He supported the views of the man whose room he tended.

Read this passage. The sentences are numbered. Answer questions 18 and 19.

(1) Our school's principal, Mr. Vickers, made a special announcement this morning. (2) Mr. Vickers said that the weather had been good this past winter, and the school didn't use any of its snow days. (3) To make up for it, Parker Elementary School would be closed for an extra day next week. (4) That news had me smiling all day.

18. Which word in sentence 1 is a possessive noun?

   A school's
   B principal
   C this
   D special

19. Which of these nouns from sentence 2 is an object noun?

   A Mr. Vickers
   B weather
   C days
   D school

Read this passage from "James Madison: Father of the Constitution." Answer questions 20 and 21.

Madison was a Federalist. Federalists thought the states had too much power. Federalists wanted a strong national government. They believed such a government could protect the country and help it grow. They convinced Congress to call a convention to "fix" the [government]. But the Federalists' goal was to write a new <u>constitution</u>.

20. The Federalists thought a strong federal government would —

   A give the states too much power
   B help the whole country stay safe and thrive
   C take power away from Congress
   D help them identify the most important states

21. What does the word <u>constitution</u> mean in this passage?

   A a person who wants to be a member of the U.S. Congress
   B a place where people gather to hold a national convention
   C a document that organizes the government's power and the people's rights
   D a meeting in which people make important decisions

Read this passage from "Harriet Tubman Leads the Way." Answer questions 22 and 23.

> Harriet Tubman was born a slave on the Eastern Shore, near Bucktown, Maryland. Slave life was cruel and uncertain. Slaves worked hard for no money. They could be sold at any time, and families were often torn apart. Harriet's parents—Harriet Green and Benjamin Ross—were luckier than some couples. Even though they worked for different masters, they were often able to live near each other.

22. This passage most likely comes from —

   A an observation log
   B a newspaper article
   C a persuasive essay
   D a biography

23. Why were Harriet's parents considered lucky?

   A They usually lived in the same area.
   B They lived on the same plantation all their lives.
   C They were granted freedom near Bucktown, Maryland.
   D They owned their own plantation on the Eastern Shore.

Choose the word that best completes each sentence for questions 24 and 25.

24. A change or addition to a law is called _____.

   A a preamble
   B a bill
   C an amendment
   D an article

25. A separate section of a document is known as _____.

   A an amendment
   B an article
   C a draft
   D a constitution

Student _____ Date _____

THEME **5**

Student Theme Progress Test Record

Skills Tested	Item Numbers (cross out numbers for items answered incorrectly)	Student Score	Criterion Score	If the student scored less than the Criterion Score, use these Reteaching Tools:
Comprehension Monitor Understanding	4 6 13 17 20 23	____ of 6	5 / 6	**Monitor Understanding:** Comprehension Bridge 5
Determine Importance	12 15	____ of 2	1 / 2	**Determine Importance:** Comprehension Bridge 4
Vocabulary	2 9 21 24 25	____ of 5	4 / 5	**Vocabulary:** During independent reading time, review student's Vocabulary Journal and discuss how to improve the journal entries
Word Study Synonyms and Antonyms	1 8 11	____ of 3	2 / 3	**Synonyms and Antonyms:** Sourcebook p. 139 Teacher's Guide p. 140
Multiple-Meaning Words	7 10 16	____ of 3	2 / 3	**Multiple-Meaning Words:** Sourcebook p. 151 Teacher's Guide p. 156
Writing: Process Writing Process: Drafting	3 14	____ of 2	1 / 2	**Process: Drafting:** Writing Bridge 9
Form: Biography	5 22	____ of 2	1 / 2	**Form: Biography:** Writing Bridge 10
Writing: Grammar Possessive Nouns	18	____ of 1	1 / 1	**Possessive Nouns:** Writing Resource Guide p. 9 Writer's Handbook p. 21
Subject and Object Nouns	19	____ of 1	1 / 1	**Subject and Object Nouns:** Writing Resource Guide p. 10 Writer's Handbook p. 21
		____ / 25	18 / 25	

Answer Key

1. A   2. D   3. B   4. C   5. A   6. D   7. B   8. C   9. D   10. C   11. A   12. A   13. B

14. C   15. C   16. B   17. D   18. A   19. C   20. B   21. C   22. D   23. A   24. C   25. B

THEME ⑥ Ongoing Test Practice

SAMPLE
Read the passage. Then answer the question.

Marta has many friends. It seems like there is always someone who wants to spend time with her. When her class voted on a new president, Marta got the most votes. Just about everybody likes Marta.

S. Which sentence best synthesizes the information in this passage?

A Marta is a very quiet and shy person.
B Marta enjoys spending time with her friends.
C Marta is a very popular person.
D Marta enjoys being class president.

Read the passage. Then read each question. Circle the letter of the correct answer.

Our Nation's Capital

A capital is the city where you will find the government offices of a state or country. The capital of the state of Florida is the city of Tallahassee. The capital of the country of France is the city of Paris. Washington, D.C., is the capital of the United States, but other cities have also been the home of our federal government.

When the Constitution was adopted, the first capital of the United States was New York City. Congress met in a building that had once been New York's City Hall. When the Revolutionary War ended, the building was made larger, and its name was changed to Federal Hall. The members of the first Congress under the Constitution held their initial meeting on March 4, 1789. While their main job was to create laws, their first task that day was to count votes to <u>elect</u> the president. George Washington had the most votes, and on April 30, 1789, he took the oath of office on the balcony of Federal Hall.

After Washington became president, one of his first duties was to help decide where the permanent capital would be. Many people thought that the capital should be closer to the southern states. New York City was too far away for many people in the country to travel to. After a lot of discussion, it was decided that Philadelphia, Pennsylvania, would be the capital. Ten years later, a new location on the Potomac River, which was closer to the middle of the country, became the capital.

President Washington mapped out an area that included parts of Maryland and Virginia. At the time, this land was mostly farms and swamps. In 1791 it was named the District of Columbia, and the city that was built there was called Washington, in honor of the president. By 1800, when the city officially became the capital, only part of the capitol building was ready. The president's house, which later became known as the White House, also was not finished, but it was safe enough to move into. The first person to live there was our second president, John Adams.

Today, Washington, D.C., is a major city. It is home to all three branches of government, and it is the site of many museums, monuments, and libraries. Thanks to modern cars, trains, and airplanes, it is much easier and faster for people to travel to the capital. Our government will likely remain there for many years to come.

1. Based on information in the first paragraph, you can determine that —

   A the city of Paris was once the capital of the United States
   B each of the 50 U.S. states has its own capital
   C there is a city in Florida called Washington
   D Washington, D.C., has always been the capital of the United States

2. Which of the following words from this passage are homonyms?

   A *their* and *there*
   B *state* and *country*
   C *first* and *initial*
   D *part* and *all*

3. Where was George Washington officially elected president?

   A Washington, D.C.
   B Philadelphia
   C New York City
   D Tallahassee

4. What new idea can you form based on information in paragraph 4 of this passage?

   A The members of Congress hold their meetings at the White House.
   B George Washington wanted to live in the capitol building.
   C John Adams was a better president than George Washington.
   D The president's house was not always known as the White House.

5. In this passage, the word <u>elect</u> means —

   A choose someone for office by voting
   B change the location of a meeting
   C create laws based on public opinion
   D count out the number of tasks that must be completed

Answer the following question on a separate sheet of paper.

6. Based on information in the passage, why was Philadelphia probably the capital of the United States for only ten years?

THEME **6** Theme Progress Test

Read each question. Fill in the correct circle on your answer document.

1. When you write, transition words should be used to —

   A make your writing more descriptive
   B explain the meaning of a new word
   C support your main idea
   D move from one idea to the next

2. When you synthesize as you read, you —

   A determine the meaning of new words
   B use information in the text to develop a new idea
   C identify the most important detail in the text
   D stop and review what you have read to make sure you understand

3. Which of these words is a homonym for the word *tale*?

   A tail
   B story
   C sale
   D truth

4. What does the word <u>conclude</u> mean in the sentence below?

   > After hearing Basil's story and discussing what happened, I can <u>conclude</u> that he did the right thing.

   A describe a series of events
   B listen to a person tell a story
   C form an opinion about something
   D ask questions about something

5. What usually happens at the beginning of a story?

   A The solution to the main problem in the story is explained.
   B The main problem or conflict in the story is described.
   C The resolution to the main conflict in the story is described.
   D The main conflict in the story is explored in greater detail.

6. Read this passage from "Being a Judge: An Interview with Julia Packard."

> I may have ten cases per month, and I hear cases only three or four days of the month. All the rest of my time is spent either on the telephone talking to people involved in a case or writing decisions. If we can settle things over the telephone, people may not have to come to court. Once I have made a decision, I have to write it out in detail. So the biggest part of each month is spent writing.

Why does the judge in this passage spend a lot of time on the telephone?

A She has to tell people when to come to court and what to bring with them.

B She calls other judges to see what they think about her cases.

C She tries to resolve problems so people do not have to go to court.

D She tries to find people who would like to be members of a jury.

7. Which words in the sentence below are verbs?

> The students sat in a circle on the floor as the librarian explained how the Dewey decimal system works.

A *students, librarian, Dewey*

B *in, as, how*

C *circle, floor, system*

D *sat, explained, works*

8. Read this passage from "An Important Debate."

> *CONGRESSMAN ROCK:* Thank you, Mister Speaker. There are two good reasons for keeping the dams. They generate electricity, and they have made it possible for freight barges to travel all the way to Lewiston, Idaho. Barge traffic has greatly boosted the economy of Lewiston, making it a seaport. Then, too, the dams have not harmed the salmon in the river in any major way. It makes no sense to remove the dams.

You can tell from the passage that Congressman Rock believes that —

A only some of the dams should be removed

B the dams are beneficial and should not be removed

C salmon traffic is harming dams in Lewiston

D freight barges have caused a lot of pollution in Lewiston

9. Which of these words is a homonym for the word *sights*?

A lights

B sites

C places

D sounds

10. Read this passage. The sentences are numbered.

> (1) Logan's uncle had taught her to play chess during her last visit. (2) Logan looked forward to a fun weekend playing chess with her aunt and uncle. (3) Since then, chess had been her favorite game. (4) Logan was going to visit her aunt and uncle for the weekend.

What is the best way to reorganize the sentences in this passage?

A switch sentences 1 and 4

B 4, 1, 3, 2

C switch sentences 3 and 4

D 2, 3, 1, 4

11. Which of these words is a homonym of the word *root*?

A cheer

B stem

C route

D loot

12. Which list of words contains all verbs?

A happily, thoughtfully, knowingly

B angry, courteous, doubtful

C wallet, notebook, stove

D consider, respond, describe

13. Read this passage from "Being a Judge: An Interview with Julia Packard."

> To become a federal judge, you must first be a lawyer. So the first thing you have to do if you want to be a federal judge is go to law school. Then you must be interested in settling arguments between people—that is the main part of the job. You want to make the two sides happy in a case, but that isn't always possible. You must be able to decide which person has the law on his or her side.

What new idea can you form when synthesizing the information in this passage?

A If a person doesn't like the way a case ends, he or she can ask the judge to reconsider it.

B Everyone who goes to law school gets to be a federal judge.

C The person who has the law on his or her side will probably win the case.

D If you lose a case in court, you cannot become a federal judge.

Choose the word that best completes each sentence for questions 14 and 15.

14. When you name someone as a candidate for a position, you _____ him or her.

    A nominate
    B elect
    C appoint
    D conclude

15. The branch of government responsible for interpreting laws in court is the _____ branch.

    A Congress
    B legislative
    C executive
    D judicial

Read these lines from the poem "A Three-Part Masterpiece." Answer questions 16 and 17.

> 1600 Pennsylvania Avenue—the White House
> Its East and West Wings cradling a strong center
> Mirroring the three branches of government
> Home to America's presidents who
> <u>Enforce</u> her laws, design her policies, command her armies—
> 1600 Pennsylvania Avenue
> Seat of power

16. The ideas in this poem help you understand that —

    A the president gets to decide who will make the laws
    B the president is the most important leader in the world
    C the White House is where the president lives and works
    D the three branches of government are located in the White House

17. What does the word <u>enforce</u> mean in this poem?

    A create a new law
    B make sure people obey a law
    C decide whether a law is fair
    D make changes to a law

Read this passage from "Guess Who's Home." Answer questions 18 and 19.

> Isabel looked up from the portrait she'd been studying in the Green Room of the White House. She must have been daydreaming. Her class had already moved on to the next room of their White House tour. Isabel and Leah ran to catch up with them. They found themselves looking into a huge open room with glittering crystal chandeliers. Their teacher, Mrs. Morris, was saying to the class, "The President uses the East Room for large social gatherings and ceremonies."

18. Where does this passage take place?

    A at the White House

    B in an art gallery

    C at a ceremony

    D in a classroom

19. What new idea can you synthesize based on this passage?

    A Isabel's class is in a hurry to finish their tour of the White House.

    B Isabel is distracted by the glittering chandeliers and gets left behind by her class.

    C Isabel's class has been invited to a party in the East Room of the White House.

    D Social gatherings at the White House are probably very formal.

Read this passage from "An Important Debate." Answer questions 20 and 21.

> And, finally, the dams do indeed hurt the salmon. They make it very difficult for young salmon to reach the sea. Those that do make it often cannot get back to their breeding grounds upriver. Salmon have almost vanished from the Snake River. I think it's clear that the dams must be removed.

20. Which of the following best describes how the ideas in this passage are organized?

    A in the order that events occurred

    B from the most important idea to the least important idea

    C from the least important idea to the most important idea

    D from problem to solution

21. The ideas in this passage help you understand that —

    A the Snake River is an ideal place to build more dams

    B the salmon in the Snake River are harming the dams

    C removing the dams will help increase the number of salmon

    D salmon are strong fish that can survive in harsh conditions

Read this passage from "Guess Who's Home." Answer questions 22 and 23.

> Suddenly, Isabel jerked out of her daydream and realized that the room was empty and eerily quiet. Her class had vanished. Panicked, Isabel turned and ran into the hallway to find them, frantically dashing from room to room, up and down hallways, her heart pounding. She ducked under a barricade and darted up a flight of stairs. At the top, Isabel turned a corner and started down another hallway. When she heard voices, she looked up. It took her a second to realize what she was seeing, but when she did, she stopped in her tracks.
>
> "Mr. President," she whispered. He stopped, too, staring at Isabel.

22. What is the setting of the events in this passage?

   A a large outdoor meeting

   B a small house

   C a classroom

   D a large building

23. What new idea can you form based on the information in this passage?

   A Isabel went somewhere she was not supposed to go.

   B Isabel wants to become president when she grows up.

   C Isabel spends a lot of time daydreaming.

   D Isabel scared the president when she met him.

Read this passage. The sentences are numbered. Answer questions 24 and 25.

> (1) Helena stood at the foul line with the basketball clenched tightly in her hands. (2) She had two chances to shoot the ball. (3) If she made both baskets, her team would win the game. (4) Helena felt the pressure, but she remained confident. (5) She knew she could do it.

24. Which of these words from sentence 1 is a noun?

   A *stood*   **C** *clenched*

   B *line*   **D** *tightly*

25. Which word in sentence 4 is a linking verb?

   A *felt*   **C** *but*

   B *pressure*   **D** *confident*

Student _____ Date _____

Student Theme Progress Test Record

Skills Tested	Item Numbers (cross out numbers for items answered incorrectly)	Student Score	Criterion Score	If the student scored less than the Criterion Score, use these Reteaching Tools:
Comprehension Synthesize	2 13 16 19 21 23	_____ of 6	5 / 6	**Synthesize:** Comprehension Bridge 6
Monitor Understanding	6 8	_____ of 2	1 / 2	**Monitor Understanding:** Comprehension Bridge 5
Target Skill Identify Story Structure	5	_____ of 1	1 / 1	**Identify Story Structure:** Teacher's Guide p. 181
Identify Setting	18 22	_____ of 2	1 / 2	**Identify Setting:** Teacher's Guide p. 190
Vocabulary	4 14 15 17	_____ of 4	3 / 4	**Vocabulary:** During independent reading time, review student's Vocabulary Journal and discuss how to improve the journal entries
Word Study Homonyms	3 9 11	_____ of 3	2 / 3	**Homonyms:** Sourcebook p. 169 Teacher's Guide p. 172
Writing: Process Writing Trait: Organization	1 10	_____ of 2	1 / 2	**Trait: Organization:** Writing Bridge 11
Organizational Pattern: Problem and Solution	20	_____ of 1	1 / 1	**Organizational Pattern: Problem and Solution:** Writing Bridge 12
Writing: Grammar Action and Linking Verbs	25	_____ of 1	1 / 1	**Action and Linking Verbs:** Writing Resource Guide p. 12 Writer's Handbook p. 23
Review Nouns	24	_____ of 1	1 / 1	**Nouns:** Writing Resource Guide p. 11 Writer's Handbook p. 20
Verbs	7 12	_____ of 2	1 / 2	**Verbs:** Writing Resource Guide p. 16 Writer's Handbook p. 23
		_____ / 25	18 / 25	

Answer Key

1. D 2. B 3. A 4. C 5. B 6. C 7. D 8. B 9. B 10. B 11. C 12. D 13. C

14. A 15. D 16. C 17. B 18. A 19. D 20. D 21. C 22. D 23. A 24. B 25. A

Name _____ Date _____

SAMPLE

Read the passage. Then answer the question.

Jaime's eyes were shut tight, and his heart was pounding in his chest. He had butterflies in his stomach as the car crept to the top of the track. Then he screamed as the cars rocketed down the long, steep slope. Jaime loved roller coasters.

S. The writer of this passage wants you to imagine —

   A what Jaime felt

   B how Jaime sat

   C what Jaime heard

   D what Jaime saw

Read the passage. Then read each question. Circle the letter of the correct answer.

Yera Can't Sleep

Yera was trying to get some sleep, but the restaurant down the block was keeping him up. The bright glow from its sign shone through Yera's window. The music from the restaurant thumped in Yera's head as he covered himself with blankets. "How am I supposed to get any sleep?" he groaned.

The next morning, Yera stumbled into the kitchen. "You look terrible," his mother said. "Didn't you get any sleep last night?"

"Not really," Yera replied with a yawn. "The light and noise from that restaurant down the street kept me up again."

"That place shouldn't be open so late at night," his sister, Naja, said. "There should be a law against being open that late."

"You're right," Yera said. "Dad, will you take me to a city council meeting?"

"Sure," his father answered. "There's a meeting next Thursday. But if you want the city to make a new law, you will have to explain what the law should do and why it should be passed."

For the next few days, Yera worked on a report for the city council meeting. He realized that he couldn't ask the city to close the restaurant. The owners had a right to do business, and many people in town liked to eat there. Instead, he decided to propose a curfew for noisy businesses on weeknights. This was not a <u>unique</u> request. Many cities all over the country had similar laws. Yera just hoped the city council would agree with him.

The night of the meeting, Yera put on his fancy blue suit with his best white shirt and a dark red tie. He gathered his notes and put them in a brand new pocket folder.

When Yera and his family arrived at city hall, they sat quietly in the audience. Yera's stomach tingled, and his throat was scratchy and dry. When it was his turn to speak, Yera got up and read his presentation. His voice cracked and his hands shook, but by the time he finished his speech, many people were nodding their heads.

"This sounds like a serious issue that affects many people," said the city council leader. "We will consider your statement and hold a public hearing. You made a great speech and presented a strong case!"

Yera couldn't help but smile.

1. Based on information in the passage, how does Yera probably feel after his speech?

   A exhausted
   B embarrassed
   C disappointed
   D proud

2. Which word best describes the mood of paragraph 2 of the passage?

   A playful
   B weary
   C thoughtful
   D cheerful

3. What does the word <u>unique</u> mean in this passage?

   A unusual
   B noisy
   C common
   D difficult

4. In the first paragraph, why does the author describe the light and sounds from the restaurant?

   A so you know what kind of food the restaurant serves
   B so you can figure out where Yera likes to eat
   C so you can imagine why Yera cannot get to sleep
   D so you know what time Yera goes to bed

5. Which detail from the passage best helps you picture how Yera feels during his speech?

   A Yera is with his family.
   B Many people nod their heads.
   C Yera's hands are shaking.
   D Yera is standing in the audience.

Answer the following question on a separate sheet of paper.

6. Use your imagination and information from the passage to describe how Yera feels as he gets ready for the city council meeting.

THEME 7 Theme Progress Test

Read each question. Fill in the correct circle on your answer document.

1. Which word in the sentence below is a helping verb?

> Callie and Maria had planned to spend the weekend working on their science project.

   A had
   B spend
   C working
   D their

2. What does it mean to create images when you read?

   A identify the beginning, middle, and end of a passage
   B think about how things look, sound, feel, smell, and taste
   C look for clues about where and when the passage takes place
   D decide whether information in the passage is important

3. What does the word <u>plankton</u> mean in the sentence below?

> <u>Plankton</u> are swept from place to place by the ocean current and provide nutrition for most aquatic life.

   A pebbles, sand, and sticks at the bottom of the ocean
   B people who work on fishing boats far out in the ocean
   C tiny plants and animals that serve as food for sea creatures
   D large fish that are usually found near the seashore

4. Which words in the sentence below are helping verbs?

> The children had hoped they would be going to the circus, but they were taking a trip to the zoo instead.

   A had, would, were
   B hoped, going, taking
   C they, but, instead
   D children, circus, zoo

5. Which word in the sentence below is a linking verb?

> Kosal looked tired because he stayed up all night studying for the big test.

A tired   **C** studying

B stayed   **D** looked

6. Read this passage from "Squid Attack!"

> Rollie checked the submersible's control panel to make sure his microphone was turned off, then he sighed heavily. "Come on, Rollie," he said aloud. "Get a grip on yourself. You've done this dozens of times—one bad experience doesn't change all the others."

Which of the following details from the passage helps you understand how Rollie feels?

A Rollie has had the same experience dozens of times.

B Rollie makes sure the microphone is off.

C Rollie checks the control panel.

D Rollie sighs heavily.

7. Which of the following best describes a newspaper article?

A A newspaper article explains how to complete a task.

B A newspaper article includes facts that answer the questions *Who? What? Where? When?* and *Why?*

C A newspaper article provides definitions for many words.

D A newspaper article tells a story about made-up characters.

8. If you write a story about your life to read to your friends, you should —

A include many difficult words and phrases

B use words and phrases that reflect your personality

C write about events from several different viewpoints

D describe what your friends want to do when they grow up

9. Which of these lists contains words that are all helping verbs?

A write, relax, wander

B friendly, young, careful

C could, must, did

D glance, share, resist

10. Read this sentence.

> Bryan <u>was</u> the first in his family to go to college.

The verb <u>was</u> connects which two words in this sentence?

A Bryan, first
B first, family
C family, college
D Bryan, college

11. Read this passage from "Dr. Sylvia Earle."

> Dr. Earle is interested in all aspects of ocean life. She once lived in a small structure in the ocean for two weeks! The underwater home even had a living room with a television. No one really watched it, according to Dr. Earle. She claims the best show was happening outside. Dr. Earle recalls not wanting to sleep so she could spend more time in the water with the brightly colored fish.

Which word best describes the mood of this passage?

A serious
B dark
C sad
D cheerful

Choose the word that best completes each sentence for questions 12 and 13.

12. Many animals have skeletons that are made partly of bone and partly of _____.

A chlorophyll
B cartilage
C marine
D competition

13. When you connect two things, you _____ them to each other.

A attach
B section
C inhabit
D marine

Read this passage from "Ocean Census Half-Completed." Answer questions 14 and 15.

> **Ocean Census Half-Completed**
> *by David L. Dreier*
> Washington, D.C.—Do you think the oceans have been explored? If you do, think again. Scientists have studied only a small part of the ocean depths. The Census of <u>Marine</u> Life—a massive 10-year study—hopes to change this. Project leaders recently updated reporters on the project's goals and progress.

14. How do you know this passage came from a newspaper article?

   A The passage was written in Washington, D.C.

   B The passage mentions a massive 10-year study.

   C The passage has a headline and contains facts about a recent event.

   D The passage identifies different types of people, including scientists and reporters.

15. What does the word <u>marine</u> refer to in this passage?

   A people who count living things

   B reporters who work in Washington, D.C.

   C people who study the ocean

   D animals and plants that live in the sea

Read this passage from "Squid Attack!" Answer questions 16 and 17.

> He stared down at *Izzy*, his individual submersible deep-sea vessel. He had always loved climbing into the sub's cramped interior and diving thousands of feet below the surface of the ocean. Now he could barely endure the sight of its domed top. The thought of sliding down into the steel shell and pulling the hatch closed made his knees feel weak.

16. Which words in the passage help you imagine what the submersible deep-sea vessel looks like?

   A *cramped, domed, steel*

   B *climbing, diving, sliding*

   C *individual, below, knees*

   D *sight, hatch, weak*

17. Which word best describes the tone of this passage?

   A playful   C exciting

   B tense   D annoying

Read these lines from the poem "Into the Deep." Answer questions 18 and 19.

> sunlit waves winking
> twinkling rays streaming,
> sinking
> down below
> through reds and golds
> warming life that swims and grows

18. As you read this poem, you should picture —

    A how the air around the water smells

    B the temperature of the water at night

    C what water sounds like as waves break

    D how the sea looks as sunlight shines through it

19. Which word best describes the mood of this poem?

    A cheerful

    B angry

    C peaceful

    D sad

Read this passage. The sentences are numbered. Answer questions 20 and 21.

> (1) The firefighter who was driving the truck steered skillfully through the streets. (2) The siren blared, warning everyone to get out of the way. (3) As soon as they arrived, the firefighter _____ off the truck and got to work.

20. What is the main verb in sentence 1?

    A driving

    B steered

    C skillfully

    D was

21. Which verb best completes sentence 3?

    A jump

    B jumping

    C jumped

    D jumps

Read this passage from "Dr. Sylvia Earle." Answer questions 22 and 23.

Until she was a young teen, Sylvia Earle lived on a small farm in New Jersey. In summer her family often went to the shore. Earle fondly recalls these trips. She remembers on the way there first being able to smell the ocean and then hearing the water pound against the shore. After a few more minutes, she would finally see the water she loves so much.

22. Why does the writer describe what Sylvia Earle smelled, heard, and saw as she approached the ocean?

   A to help you understand how Sylvia Earle feels about the ocean
   B to identify why Sylvia Earle's family was going to the ocean
   C to describe why Sylvia Earle does not like the ocean
   D to explain where Sylvia Earle's family was traveling from

23. Which statement best describes Sylvia Earle's childhood vacations?

   A She was frightened of the ocean and dreaded going to the shore.
   B Her family lived on the shore and took trips to a small farm.
   C Her family spent summer vacations traveling outside the country.
   D She loved the summer trips her family took to the shore.

Read this passage from "Squid Attack!" Answer questions 24 and 25.

"Only a squid?" Rollie groaned. Then he gasped when he saw the giant squid's beak opening and closing in the lights . . . One of the squid's long arms was wrapped around the submersible's dome, its double rows of suckers gripping the glass. Rollie screamed again.

24. Which words from the passage best reveal how Rollie feels?

   A *opening* and *closing*
   B *gasped* and *screamed*
   C *gripping* and *giant*
   D *wrapped* and *submersible's*

25. Which sentence best synthesizes the information in this passage?

   A Rollie's submersible is being attacked by a giant squid.
   B Rollie is in a special type of ship that goes underwater.
   C The giant squid is larger than the submersible.
   D The squid has two rows of suckers on its tentacles.

Student _____ Date _____

THEME 7

Student Theme Progress Test Record

Skills Tested	Item Numbers (cross out numbers for items answered incorrectly)	Student Score	Criterion Score	If the student scored less than the Criterion Score, use these Reteaching Tools:
Comprehension Create Images	2 6 16 18 22 24	_____ of 6	5 / 6	**Create Images:** Comprehension Bridge 7
Synthesize	23 25	_____ of 2	1 / 2	**Synthesize:** Comprehension Bridge 6
Target Skill Identify Tone/Mood	11 17 19	_____ of 3	2 / 3	**Identify Tone/Mood:** Teacher's Guide p. 224
Vocabulary	3 12 13 15	_____ of 4	3 / 4	**Vocabulary:** During independent reading time, review student's Vocabulary Journal and discuss how to improve the journal entries
Writing: Process Writing Trait: Voice	8	_____ of 1	1 / 1	**Trait: Voice:** Writing Bridge 13
Form: Newspaper Article	7 14	_____ of 2	1 / 2	**Form: Newspaper Article:** Writing Bridge 14
Writing: Grammar Linking Verbs	5 10	_____ of 2	1 / 2	**Linking Verbs:** Writing Resource Guide p. 12 Writer's Handbook p. 24
Main and Helping Verbs	1 4 9 20	_____ of 4	3 / 4	**Main and Helping Verbs:** Writing Resource Guide p. 13 Writer's Handbook p. 24
Past, Present, and Future Verb Tenses	21	_____ of 1	1 / 1	**Past, Present, and Future Verb Tenses:** Writing Resource Guide p. 14 Writer's Handbook p. 26
		_____ / 25	18 / 25	

Answer Key

1. A   **2.** B   **3.** C   **4.** A   **5.** D   **6.** D   **7.** B   **8.** B   **9.** C   **10.** A   **11.** D   **12.** B   **13.** A

14. C   **15.** D   **16.** A   **17.** B   **18.** D   **19.** C   **20.** B   **21.** C   **22.** A   **23.** D   **24.** B   **25.** A

Name _____ Date _____

SAMPLE
Read the passage. Then answer the question.

The wild rafflesia is found only in certain forests. It has a strong smell like rotting meat, which helps attract flies. Its petals can grow to be several feet long, making it one of the largest flowers in the world.

S. What is a rafflesia?

A a type of meat
B a kind of animal
C a type of flower
D a kind of forest

Read the passage. Then read each question. Circle the letter of the correct answer.

Jacques Cousteau

Jacques Cousteau was born in France on June 11, 1910. Even as a child he was like a fish—he loved the water. He enjoyed swimming in lakes, rivers, and oceans, where he could see all kinds of sea life. He was also interested in machines and movies. As he got older, he spent a lot of time building things and making his own films with a home movie camera.

When he grew up, Cousteau joined the French navy. This gave him his first real chance to explore life under the sea. Cousteau knew that people could not stay submerged for a long time because they are <u>dependent</u> on air for survival. So he started working on a machine that would let him breathe while diving.

In 1943 he and a man named Emile Gagnan invented the aqualung. This new machine allowed a person to stay underwater for a few hours. When World War II ended, divers used aqualungs to find and get rid of old mines that could damage ships.

In 1948 Cousteau bought the *Calypso*. This was an old navy ship that was used as a ferry after the war. He turned the ship into his own floating research lab. Then he hired some people and went out into the ocean to make movies. Two of his best known films are *The Silent World* and *World Without Sun*. These movies helped teach people about incredible ocean creatures. They also won major awards and made Cousteau very famous.

In 1968 he made his own television show called *The Undersea World of Jacques Cousteau*. For the first time, people could see sharks, tropical fish, starfish, dolphins, and whales in their homes every week. The program lasted eight years.

Cousteau used his fame to help raise funds for the Cousteau Society. This organization used the money to help keep the oceans clean and safe for sea creatures. Over time more than 300,000 people joined the group.

Even after his show ended, Cousteau regularly set sail in the *Calypso* to explore and to make movies. On January 11, 1996, the *Calypso* was hit by another boat in Singapore harbor and sank. Just over a year later, on June 25, 1997, Cousteau passed away. Although he is gone, Cousteau remains an important figure in oceanography.

1. You can tell from the passage that an *aqualung* is —

   A a special movie camera that works underwater
   B a type of ship used by France during World War II
   C a type of fish found near France
   D a machine that lets people breathe underwater

2. What does the word <u>dependent</u> mean in this passage?

   A to breathe
   B to rely on something
   C to hold your breath
   D to want something

3. In paragraph 6 of the passage, what does the word *funds* mean?

   A money
   B awareness
   C membership
   D pollution

4. Read this sentence from the passage.

   > He knew that people could not stay submerged for a long time because they need air.

   Using information from the passage, you can figure out that *submerged* means —

   A in a movie
   B on a ship
   C under the water
   D near a shark

5. Which of these sentences from the passage contains a simile?

   A *Even as a child he was like a fish—he loved the water.*
   B *Over time more than 300,000 people joined the group.*
   C *He turned the ship into his own floating research lab.*
   D *When he grew up, Cousteau joined the French navy.*

Answer the following question on a separate sheet of paper.

6. Using information from the passage, explain what *oceanography* is.

THEME ⑧ Theme Progress Test

Read each question. Fill in the correct circle on your answer document.

1. What does it mean to use fix-up strategies as you read?

   A connect ideas in a passage to what you already know

   B use information in a passage to develop a new idea

   C bring together similar ideas in a passage to create a summary

   D use information in a passage to figure out the meaning of a new word

2. Which of these verbs is written in the present tense?

   A wrote   **C** danced

   B tosses   **D** threw

3. Read this passage from "Why the Lanternfish Gives Off Light—A Cajun Folktale."

   > Fish didn't realize that the brilliant pearls he had swallowed were shining through his scales. And that is why today the luminous lanternfish of the deep gives off light.

   By reading on, you can figure out that *luminous* means —

   A heavy   **C** tiny

   B glowing   **D** slippery

4. Which of these words in the sentence below is an adjective?

   > The attentive gardener carefully inspected every flower in the garden.

   A every   **C** carefully

   B gardener   **D** inspected

5. Read this passage from "The Adventures of Hercules on Sea and Land."

   > He said, "Everyone knows of my greatness. What does the unworthy son of Zeus want from me?"

   By breaking the word *unworthy* into parts, you can figure out that it means —

   A great   **C** not deserving

   B lucky   **D** very deserving

6. Read this passage from "The Mariana Trench."

> The plates float on hot liquid rock, called "magma." Since the continents and oceans are on top of the plates, the shape of the land and water changes as the plates move.

How is this passage organized?

A problem to solution   C order of events

B cause and effect   D compare and contrast

7. Read this passage from "Why the Lanternfish Gives Off Light—A Cajun Folktale."

> The Gulf of Mexico grew darker and darker, and eventually there was no light at all. The marine creatures ran into rocks, shells, and even each other in the dark! Most decided to move closer to the surface of the water, where there was more light. Fish, however, was too stubborn to move.
>
> "Dis is my home," Fish proclaimed defiantly.

Which sentence from this passage contains dialect?

A *The Gulf of Mexico grew darker and darker, and eventually there was no light at all.*

B *Most decided to move closer to the surface of the water, where there was more light.*

C *Fish, however, was too stubborn to move.*

D *"Dis is my home," Fish proclaimed defiantly.*

8. Read this passage. The sentences are numbered.

> (1) The animals that make up coral reefs are called polyps. (2) Polyps are encased by coral skeletons. (3) Large groups of coral look like underwater bushes.

Which sentence should be added after sentence 2?

A Coral skeletons build and grow on top of one another.

B Coral reefs are found only in warm, shallow water.

C Many tropical fish live in and around a coral reef.

D Pollution is the biggest threat to the survival of coral reefs.

9. Choose the word that best completes this sentence.

> Victoria _____ her favorite poem and read it to her class last week.

A memorize   C memorized

B memorizes   D memorizing

10. What does the word <u>conserve</u> mean in the sentence below?

> We have not had a lot of rain this year, so the city is asking everyone to <u>conserve</u> water.

A use all at once

B stop using

C use as much as possible

D use as little as possible

11. Read this passage from "The Adventures of Hercules on Sea and Land."

> Hercules found Atlas and offered to take his load if Atlas fetched the apples. Atlas had been holding the Earth and Sky for so long that he was thrilled to have Hercules offer some relief. Atlas gave the Sky and Earth to Hercules, and shortly after, he returned with the golden apples.

By reading on, you can figure out that the word *fetched* means —

A gave someone a break from work

B held something very heavy

C went to get something

D made someone feel better

12. Read this passage.

> (1) Martina walked slowly up the walkway to the front door. (2) She was very nervous because she had never tried to sell anything before. (3) Finally a little boy stuck his head out the window and said, "Sorry, lady, we're not home!" (4) Nothing happened. (5) She knocked and then waited for someone to answer.

What is the best way to improve this passage?

A add a sentence about where Martina lives

B switch sentences 3 and 5

C delete sentence 1

D switch sentences 2 and 3

13. Which word from the sentence below is NOT an adjective?

> The new student carefully studied the large classroom to determine where he should sit.

A where   **C** new

B the   **D** large

14. Read this passage from "Why the Lanternfish Gives Off Light—A Cajun Folktale."

> But Fish's young son felt quite differently. T-Fish pleaded, "Please, Daddy. I want to go up dare. I'm terribly scared of da dark!"

Which phrase from this passage is an example of dialect?

A *felt quite differently*

B *T-Fish pleaded*

C *I want to go*

D *scared of da dark*

15. Which of the following lists of words contains all adjectives?

A calendar, automobile, radio

B enormous, smelly, silent

C raise, follow, explain

D slowly, cautiously, thankfully

Read these lines from "Going, Going, Gone?" Answer questions 16 and 17.

> I dreamed I swam with [a rare] hake.
> Its black-blue body
> was like the midnight sky.
> Going, going, gone. . . .
>
> I saw a huge net coming at me
> like a giant hand.
> "Look out!" I cried aloud.

16. Based on these lines from the poem, you can tell that a *hake* is —

A a type of bird

B an ocean current

C a type of fish

D a type of star

17. Which of the following includes a simile?

A *I dreamed I swam with [a rare] hake.*

B *Its blue-black body was like the midnight sky.*

C *"Look out!" I cried aloud.*

D *I saw a huge net coming at me.*

Read this passage from "The Mariana Trench." Answer questions 18 and 19.

> Earth is an amazing place. You may have heard about Earth's scorching hot deserts and polar ice caps. You may have read stories about the prairies and rain forests. You may have seen pictures of towering mountains such as Mount Everest. Maybe you have even visited deep, rocky canyons such as the Grand Canyon.

18. Which words help you imagine Earth's amazing places?

    A *place, amazing, stories*
    B *visited, pictures, caps*
    C *read, seen, heard*
    D *scorching, towering, polar*

19. What does the word *scorching* mean in this passage?

    A very sandy
    B very dry
    C very hot
    D very cold

Read this passage. The sentences are numbered. Answer questions 20 and 21.

> (1) The light bulb in the closet stopped working, so Hala had to _____ it. (2) First she unscrewed it and shook it to see if it was really broken. (3) She heard a jingle and knew a replacement was needed. (4) She took a new bulb out of the package and screwed it in carefully. (5) When she flipped the switch on the wall, the closet filled with light.

20. Which word best completes sentence 1?

    A change
    B changes
    C changed
    D changing

21. Which of these words from the passage is an irregular verb?

    A really
    B bulb
    C shook
    D flipped

Choose the word that best completes each sentence for questions 22 and 23.

22. The tree frog's bright green skin acts as _____ because it helps the frog hide on leaves.

   A an environment
   B a niche
   C a depth
   D a camouflage

23. If something is _____, you can see right through it.

   A beneath
   B transparent
   C endangered
   D dependent

Read this passage from "The Adventures of Hercules on Sea and Land." Answer questions 24 and 25.

Nereus laughed loudly. He said, "I hope you have to scavenge all over the Earth and never find the garden. It would be a pleasure to see a mighty man like Hercules fail!"

In anger, Hercules grabbed Nereus. He demanded that the sea god tell him the location. But Nereus had many tricks. The sea god quickly changed himself into a giant squid. With his many arms, he grabbed Hercules and pulled him down to the deepest depths of the sea.

A giant squid is strong enough to strangle a whale. However, Nereus was no match for Hercules. Even after being dragged a mile underwater in the ocean, Hercules hung on tightly and wrestled the giant sea monster.

24. Which words from the passage help you picture the squid in your mind?

   A *giant, many arms, strong*
   B *sea god, location, laughed*
   C *pleasure, all over, deepest*
   D *dragged, garden, hung on*

25. What does the word scavenge mean in this passage?

   A locate   **C** search
   B wander   **D** succeed

Student _____ Date _____

THEME 8

Student Theme Progress Test Record

Skills Tested	Item Numbers (cross out numbers for items answered incorrectly)	Student Score	Criterion Score	If the student scored less than the Criterion Score, use these Reteaching Tools:
Comprehension Use Fix-Up Strategies	1 3 5 11 16 19	____ of 6	5 / 6	**Use Fix-Up Strategies:** Comprehension Bridge 8
Create Images	18 24	____ of 2	1 / 2	**Create Images:** Comprehension Bridge 7
Target Skill Recognize Dialect	7 14	____ of 2	1 / 2	**Recognize Dialect:** Teacher's Guide p. 247
Understand Simile	17	____ of 1	1 / 1	**Understand Simile:** Teacher's Guide p. 256
Vocabulary	10 22 23 25	____ of 4	3 / 4	**Vocabulary:** During independent reading time, review student's Vocabulary Journal and discuss how to improve the journal entries
Word Study Inflected Endings -ed, -ing, and -s	2 9	____ of 2	1 / 2	**Inflected Endings -ed, -ing, and -s** Sourcebook p. 231 Teacher's Guide p. 238
Writing: Process Writing Process: Revising	8 12	____ of 2	1 / 2	**Process: Revising:** Writing Bridge 15
Organizational Pattern: Cause and Effect	6	____ of 1	1 / 1	**Organizational Pattern: Cause and Effect:** Writing Bridge 16
Writing: Grammar Adjectives	4 13 15	____ of 3	2 / 3	**Adjectives:** Writing Resource Guide p. 24 Writer's Handbook p. 26
Regular and Irregular Verbs	21	____ of 1	1 / 1	**Regular and Irregular Verbs:** Writing Resource Guide p. 15 Writer's Handbook p. 24
Review Verbs	20	____ of 1	1 / 1	**Verbs:** Writing Resource Guide p. 16 Writer's Handbook p. 23
		____ / 25	18 / 25	

Answer Key

1. D 2. B 3. B 4. A 5. C 6. B 7. D 8. A 9. C 10. D 11. C 12. B 13. A

14. D 15. B 16. C 17. B 18. D 19. C 20. A 21. C 22. D 23. B 24. A 25. C

Mid-Year Review

Read the passage. Then read each question. Fill in the correct circle on your answer document.

How the Liberty Bell Got Its Crack

There are many important symbols of the United States, including the American flag and the bald eagle. One of the best-known symbols of the United States is the Liberty Bell. What makes the Liberty Bell stand out is not its design or its size. Instead the bell is best known for being cracked. But how did the crack get there, and why is it significant?

In 1751 the Pennsylvania Assembly ordered a bell for its new State House building. A company in London, England, made the bell and then shipped it back to Pennsylvania in 1752. In 1753 workers hung the bell outside to ring it before carrying it up to the bell tower. The very first time the bell was rung, the clapper cracked the bell. So the men took the bell down and sent it to a local shop to be repaired. It had to be recast twice before it was fixed properly. When the repair was done, the bell was finally hung in the bell tower of the State House.

On July 18, 1776, the bell was rung to <u>proclaim</u> that the Declaration of Independence had been signed. From that point on, the "Old State House Bell" became a symbol of the American Revolution. In 1777 the British army moved into Philadelphia. American soldiers fought to <u>conquer</u> the British and win independence. People were worried that the British soldiers might destroy the bell, so they took it down and moved it to a nearby village. They hid the bell under the floor of a local church. When it was safe again, they brought the bell back to the State House, which became known as Independence Hall.

When the war ended in 1783, the Liberty Bell rang in celebration of England's loss. For the next few decades, the bell was rung on Independence Day and when important people died. In 1835 the bell was rung when the Chief Justice of the Supreme Court, John Marshall, died. Once again the bell cracked, and once again it was fixed.

Around this time, the anti-slavery movement was gaining strength. People began to realize that freedom was important for all people, no matter what color their skin was. A newspaper printed a poem about freedom in which the bell was called the Liberty Bell. The name stuck.

In 1846 the Liberty Bell was rung to celebrate the 100th anniversary of the birth of George Washington. Once again the bell cracked. This time the crack was so bad that the bell could not be rung again.

In 1852 the bell was taken down from the tower and placed in a special visitors' room in Independence Hall. A few years later, the government started sending the bell around the country to large fairs. Finally, in the 1930s, people decided that it was too risky to keep moving the bell.

Today the Liberty Bell is located in its own pavilion, just a short distance away from Independence Hall. Even though it has been more than 150 years since the bell was last rung, the Liberty Bell remains an important and enduring symbol of freedom.

1. Based on information in paragraph 2, you can figure out that the workers hung the bell outside because they —

   A did not want to make a lot of noise in the building

   B did not want to carry it all the way up to the bell tower

   C wanted to try to crack it before they installed it

   D wanted to test the bell before they installed it

2. What does the word <u>proclaim</u> mean in this passage?

   A to declare something unfair

   B to question something in public

   C to announce something officially

   D to suggest something quietly

3. Which of these details about the State House is most important to the main idea of the passage?

   A It is now called Independence Hall.

   B It was the original home of the Liberty Bell.

   C It is located in the city of Philadelphia.

   D It was once the home of the Pennsylvania Assembly.

4. Read this sentence from the passage.

   > It had to be recast twice before it was fixed properly.

   Which word is an antonym of the word *properly*?

   A correctly

   B incorrectly

   C carefully

   D carelessly

5. Which of the following questions might you ask to understand why John Marshall was considered an important person?

   A What does the Chief Justice of the Supreme Court do?

   B Where was John Marshall born?

   C Who became the next Chief Justice of the Supreme Court?

   D How old was John Marshall when he died?

6. What does the word <u>conquer</u> mean in this passage?

   A to join up with someone

   B to hide something

   C to overcome someone

   D to worry about something

7. Read this sentence from the passage.

> A few years later, the government started sending the bell around the country to large fairs.

Which word is a homonym of the word *fairs*?

A carnivals

B fares

C parties

D meetings

8. According to the passage, why did people decide to place the Liberty Bell in its own pavilion?

A They were afraid it would be damaged if they kept moving it.

B They wanted more people to travel to Philadelphia to see it.

C They were afraid it would get stolen if they kept moving it.

D They wanted to hang it back up inside Independence Hall.

9. Where was the Liberty Bell hidden during the Revolutionary War?

A under the floor of Independence Hall

B in London, England

C under the floor of a church

D in the attic of the State House

10. In what way are the Liberty Bell and the Statue of Liberty alike?

A Both are symbols of the United States.

B Both have large cracks in them.

C Both were originally located in Independence Hall.

D Both were gifts from France.

11. How is the information in this passage organized?

A from the most important idea to the least important idea

B from the least important idea to the most important idea

C in the form of step-by-step instructions

D in the order events occurred

Read the passage. Then read each question. Fill in the correct circle on your answer document.

Jin and Jellybean

Jin was sitting in the living room reading a book when she heard the slam of a car door out in the driveway. Jin glanced at the clock as she stood up. "That's strange," she thought. "Mom's home a lot later than usual."

Within a few moments, Jin realized why her mother was late. When the front door opened, a frisky little puppy burst between her mother's legs and into the hallway. "You got us a dog!" Jin squealed with glee. "You're the coolest mom ever!"

"Now calm down," her mother explained. "We're just going to take care of him and train him for a little while. Jellybean here is going to be a seeing-eye dog."

Jin remembered her mother talking about the seeing-eye dog training program a few months before. Her mother's friend, Mrs. Chang, works at an agency that helps connect people who cannot see with dogs that are specially trained to help them get around safely. "Don't worry, Mom," Jin said. "We'll train Jellybean to be the greatest seeing-eye dog ever!"

Over the next few months, Jin and Jellybean were the best of friends. They spent a lot of time together playing and training. To help housebreak the puppy, Jin took him out to the backyard many times a day. She knew that puppies need a lot of time to run around. They had a great deal of fun together. Jin wished Jellybean could live with her forever.

Jin brushed Jellybean's coat every day to help him stay clean and neat. She also taught him the basic obedience commands he would need to know in order to be a well-behaved dog. Before long, he knew exactly what to do when she said "sit" or "stay." Jin and her mother also spent time training Jellybean to follow special commands that seeing-eye dogs need to know.

Finally the day came when it was time for Jellybean to leave. For Jin, those last few weeks passed much more quickly than expected. When the doorbell rang that afternoon, she felt a knot in her stomach. Her mother opened the door to let Mrs. Chang in, but Mrs. Chang wasn't alone. Another woman and a girl a few years older than Jin followed Mrs. Chang inside.

The woman introduced herself as Mrs. Garcia and said, "This is my daughter, Isabella. She lost her sight in a car accident last year. She is the person who you've been training Jellybean for."

"Hello, Jin," Isabella said. "Thank you for taking such good care of Jellybean. I think he and I are going to be good friends." Then she turned to her mother and asked, "Mom, would it be OK if Jin comes over to visit Jellybean sometimes?"

"I think that's a wonderful idea," Mrs. Garcia said. Jin smiled and nodded her head in agreement.

12. What do Jin and Isabella have in common?

   A They are sisters.
   B They are the same age.
   C They both like Jellybean.
   D They both trained Jellybean.

13. At the end of this passage, you learn —

   A how the main problem in the story is resolved
   B where the events in the story take place
   C the names of the main characters in the story
   D when the events in the story take place

14. How do you know this story is told from the third-person point of view?

   A The narrator is one of the characters.
   B The narrator describes events but is not a character in the passage.
   C The reader is a character in the passage.
   D The narrator does not know what the characters are thinking.

15. What is the most important information about Jellybean given in the passage?

   A Jellybean spends a lot of time in the backyard.
   B Jellybean comes home with Jin's mother one day.
   C Jellybean learns how to sit on command.
   D Jellybean is going to be a seeing-eye dog for Isabella.

16. Where does this story mainly take place?

   A at a community center
   B in a park
   C in an apartment building
   D in a house

17. Why does Isabella invite Jin to come visit Jellybean?

   A Isabella and Jin are good friends who like to visit each other.
   B Isabella knows that Jin is going to miss her friend Jellybean.
   C Isabella is afraid that Jellybean will not obey anyone but Jin.
   D Isabella hopes that Jin will come over to train more dogs for her.

18. Which of these sentences from the passage includes an example of slang?

   A *"You're the coolest mom ever!"*
   B *"Mom's home a lot later than usual."*
   C *"Jellybean here is going to be a seeing-eye dog."*
   D *"She lost her sight in a car accident last year."*

19. When the doorbell rings in paragraph 7, the author wants you to imagine what Jin is —

   A seeing
   B tasting
   C feeling
   D touching

Read the passage. Then read each question. Fill in the correct circle on your answer document.

Giraffes

The giraffe is an unusual animal that has the strong body of a camel and the spotted coat of a leopard. In fact, this animal was known as a "camelopard" for many centuries. The most noticeable feature of the giraffe is its very long neck, which makes it the tallest of the land animals.

How did the giraffe get such a long neck? Nobody knows for sure. Long ago a French scientist stated that the giraffe once had a short neck like other animals. He said that over time, it had to adapt to its <u>environment</u>, so its neck grew long from stretching up to eat the leaves on the top branches of trees. Most scientists disagree with this theory.

While the giraffe's neck makes it easy for the animal to eat leaves at the top of a tree, it also makes it difficult to drink. If a giraffe wants some water, it has to spread its legs far apart so that its head can reach the ground.

A giraffe gets food and water into its mouth with its unusually large tongue. The tongue of a giraffe is about 18 inches long and can wrap around leaves and branches to pull them into the animal's mouth. A giraffe's tongue is a very dark blue color, which helps protect it from harmful solar rays that could burn it. The giraffe also has a long, strong upper lip, which helps it pull leaves from trees. It eats up to 140 pounds of food each day.

A giraffe usually grows to be about 15 to 17 feet tall and can weigh between 1,700 and 4,200 pounds. Dark spots cover most of a giraffe's body, except its belly. This animal also has small furry horns on the top of its head and long, narrow ears that stick out on the sides. Its elongated head looks like a cross between the head of a horse and the head of a camel.

A newborn giraffe, or calf, is between five and six feet tall. A new calf is usually able to run during its first day of life, but it is likely to spend most of its time during the first few weeks lying down. During this period, it is protected by its mother.

One unusual trait of the giraffe is that it does not need much sleep. A giraffe may sleep as <u>little</u> as ten minutes a day! Most of the time, it prefers between one and two hours of sleep. Because these animals do not sleep much, some people believe that giraffes cannot lie down or that if they do lie down, they will die. This is just a myth.

Giraffes are native to Africa, and they usually live in groups of about 12 to 15. Females often form their own group with a few young males. Other young males cluster together into small groups, while older males often live alone.

Unlike many other animals that <u>inhabit</u> the African wild, giraffes don't really have to worry about being attacked. They are as large as a small house, so most lions and wild dogs are afraid of them. They also have very keen senses, which warn them when danger is near. For this reason, many other types of animals often spend a lot of time near giraffes. They know that if the giraffes start to run, they need to hide, too.

Most of the time, giraffes choose to run away from danger rather than fight. They can run up to 35 miles per hour. That's about as fast as a car being driven through town! Despite its size, a giraffe running at top speed is as graceful as a ballerina. A giraffe is also capable of a frighteningly loud roar if it feels threatened. If a giraffe gets into a fight with another animal, it protects itself by kicking with its powerful rear legs and by using its head like a hammer. Even though giraffes are usually peaceful, they can be dangerous if they feel threatened.

20. Which of these sentences from the passage contains a simile?

  A *The most noticeable feature of the giraffe is its very long neck, which makes it the tallest of the land animals.*

  B *Despite its size, a giraffe running at top speed is as graceful as a ballerina.*

  C *Other young males cluster together into small groups, while older males often live alone.*

  D *The giraffe also has a long, strong upper lip, which helps it pull leaves from trees.*

21. Why was the giraffe called a camelopard for many years?

  A The word *giraffe* was too hard for many people to say.

  B The word *camelopard* means "very large animal."

  C People thought the giraffe was a mix between a camel and a leopard.

  D People thought the giraffe was a type of very tall camel.

22. Read this sentence from the passage.

> A giraffe's tongue is a very dark blue color, which helps protect it from harmful solar rays that could burn it.

What does the word *solar* mean in this sentence?

  A very hot

  B very dangerous

  C dark in color

  D from the sun

23. In paragraph 5, the author wants you to imagine what a giraffe —

  A sounds like

  B looks like

  C feels like

  D tastes like

24. What does the word <u>environment</u> mean in this passage?

  A the surroundings of a living thing

  B an area where there are many trees

  C the neck of an animal

  D a place where scientists work

25. Read the meanings below for the word <u>little</u>.

> **little**
> **1.** small in size **2.** young
> **3.** weak **4.** small in amount

Which meaning best fits the way <u>little</u> is used in the passage?

A meaning 1
B meaning 2
C meaning 3
D meaning 4

26. Which word from this sentence sounds most like the thing it describes?

> A giraffe is also capable of a frighteningly loud roar if it feels threatened.

A *loud*
B *capable*
C *roar*
D *frighteningly*

27. Which of the following best describes how information is organized in paragraph 9?

A by cause and effect
B in sequence
C from problem to solution
D from most important to least important information

28. What does the word <u>inhabit</u> mean in this passage?

A to sense danger
B to roam around
C to live in a place
D to run away

29. What question might you ask to better understand why the mother protects the calf during the first few weeks?

A How many calves does a giraffe have at one time?
B How strong is a newborn calf?
C Where does a calf prefer to lie down?
D How much does a newborn calf weigh?

30. Which sentence best synthesizes paragraph 10?

A Giraffes are very aggressive and enjoy fighting other large animals.
B The giraffe is one of the fastest animals because it has very long legs.
C Even though giraffes are very large, they are not very strong, so they often run away from danger.
D Giraffes are usually safe because they can protect themselves in a fight or quickly run away.

Mid-Year Review

Extended Response Questions

1. Using information from the passage "How the Liberty Bell Got Its Crack," explain why the bell's name changed from the "Old State House Bell" to the "Liberty Bell."

2. According to the passage "Giraffes," what features make giraffes so unique?

··

Writing Prompt

Most people have a hobby or a special activity that they like to do when they have free time.

Think about a hobby that you have or a special activity that you enjoy doing.

Now write to explain what the hobby or special activity is and why you enjoy it.

Hints for responding to the writing prompt:
- Read the prompt carefully.
- Use prewriting strategies to organize your ideas.
- Include details that help explain your main idea.
- Write sentences in different ways.
- Use words that mean exactly what you want to say.
- Look over your essay when you are done and correct any mistakes.

Mid-Year Review Test Record

Comprehension		Cross out numbers for items answered incorrectly.	
Make Connections	10 12	Monitor Understanding	9 21
Infer	1 17	Synthesize	8 30
Ask Questions	5 29	Create Images	19 23
Determine Importance	3 15	Use Fix-Up Strategies	22

If student has difficulty with Comprehension, use the Comprehension Bridges.   **Total Comprehension Score** _____ **/ 15**

Target Skills			
Recognize Onomatopoeia	26	Identify Setting	16
Identify Point of View	14	Recognize Dialect	18
Identify Story Structure	13	Understand Simile	20

If student has difficulty with Target Skills, use the Teacher's Guide lessons.   **Total Target Skills Score** _____ **/ 6**

Vocabulary

If student has difficulty with Vocabulary, review student's Vocabulary Journal.   2 6 24 28   **Total Vocabulary Score** _____ **/ 4**

Word Study			
Synonyms and Antonyms	4	Homonyms	7
Multiple-Meaning Words	25		

If student has difficulty with Word Study, use Sourcebook and Teacher's Guide lessons.   **Total Word Study Score** _____ **/ 3**

Writing: Process Writing			
Organizational Pattern: Sequence	11	Organizational Pattern: Cause and Effect	27

If student has difficulty with Process Writing, use Writing Bridges.   **Total Writing: Process Writing Score** _____ **/ 2**

           Total Score _____ **/ 30**

Answer Key

1. D	5. A	9. C	13. A	17. B	21. C	25. D	29. B
2. C	6. C	10. A	14. B	18. A	22. D	26. C	30. D
3. B	7. B	11. D	15. D	19. C	23. B	27. A	
4. B	8. A	12. C	16. D	20. B	24. A	28. C	

THEME 9 Ongoing Test Practice

SAMPLE
Read the passage. Then answer the question.

A holiday is a special day that is celebrated with one or more traditions. On Independence Day, many people watch fireworks light up the sky. On Thanksgiving, families often gather and celebrate together. On Valentine's Day, friends frequently exchange candy, cards, and flowers.

S. Which of the following is most like a holiday?

   A a birthday
   B a Saturday
   C the last day of the month
   D the first day of winter

Read the passage. Then read each question. Circle the letter of the correct answer.

Looking for Nessie

"Do you think we'll see her today?" Ricardo asked Professor Barton.

"Maybe," said Professor Barton. "You never know where or when Nessie will show up. I've waited my whole life to see her."

It was a foggy Saturday morning on the shore of a large lake in Scotland called Loch Ness. Ricardo and the professor were standing on the shore with their cameras. They scanned the lake, searching for any sign of the famed Loch Ness Monster.

"How old do you think Nessie is, Professor?" Ricardo asked.

"It's hard to say," she replied. "The first reports of a monster in the lake go back more than 1,300 years. But I don't think she's that old. If there is a creature in this water, it's probably a descendant of the original Nessie. I've never heard of an animal that could live for over a thousand years."

Then Ricardo asked, "What do you think she is? Is she a big fish? Maybe she's a really big snake or something."

The professor laughed and answered, "I doubt that Nessie is a snake, but she might be a fish. There's a type of fish called a sturgeon that can grow nearly 20 feet long. It has a long nose and spikes on its back, just like they say Nessie has. If you saw one swimming near the top of the water, you might think it was Nessie's head."

Ricardo closed his eyes and tried to imagine what a sturgeon would look like. He could understand why someone might think it was Nessie.

Professor Barton continued, "If Nessie really exists, I bet she is actually a plesiosaur. That's a type of creature that lived millions of years ago, even before the dinosaurs. It lived in the water and had a huge body, a large snout, and a very long neck, just like Nessie."

Ricardo was about to ask how a plesiosaur could still be around millions of years later when he saw something out in the water. "Look, Professor!" Ricardo shouted to his <u>companion</u>, pointing out toward the lake.

Professor Barton looked out and saw something moving in the water. They grabbed their cameras and started taking pictures. Then they heard a voice shout, "Hello!" When they looked more closely, the object seemed to be waving at them.

Much to their surprise and dismay, the "monster" in the lake turned out to be a woman paddling a canoe. The mist in the air had made it hard to see her. "Well, Ricardo," Professor Barton said, "I guess we'd better keep looking."

1. Both Ricardo and Professor Barton —

   A think Nessie is a big fish
   B believe that Nessie is not real
   C think Nessie is a plesiosaur
   D hope to see Nessie in the lake

2. In this story, Loch Ness is a symbol of —

   A mystery
   B freedom
   C happiness
   D danger

3. A plesiosaur is similar to a giraffe because both have —

   A a long nose
   B a large snout
   C a long neck
   D a huge body

4. What does the word <u>companion</u> mean in this passage?

   A a type of dinosaur
   B someone who is with you
   C a large body of water
   D someone who is paddling a canoe

5. The description of Nessie sounds most like a description of —

   A an elf
   B a dragon
   C a mermaid
   D a ghost

Answer the following question on a separate sheet of paper.

6. Based on information from the passage, in what ways are a sturgeon and a plesiosaur similar?

THEME ⑨ Theme Progress Test

Read each question. Fill in the correct circle on your answer document.

1. Which prefix do you add to the word *noticeable* to make a new word that means "not noticeable"?

   A *dis-*

   B *non-*

   C *in-*

   D *un-*

2. When you compare and contrast information in a text, you —

   A determine which information is most important

   B find similarities and differences between ideas and information

   C think about your purpose for reading

   D use different strategies to determine the meaning of a word

3. What is the best way to rewrite the sentence below?

   > Im going to invite Carol Sonya and Ellie to my house after school today!

   A I'm going to invite Carol, Sonya, and Ellie to my house after school today.

   B I'm going to invite Carol, Sonya, Ellie, to my house after school today?

   C I'm going to invite Carol; Sonya; and Ellie to my house after school today.

   D I'm going to invite Carol, Sonya, and Ellie, to my house after school today!

4. Which prefix do you add to the word *expensive* to create a new word that means "not expensive"?

   A *non-*

   B *dis-*

   C *in-*

   D *un-*

5. Which of the following best describes a symbol?

   A an object that stands for an idea or feeling

   B an object that does not really exist

   C an important character in a story

   D an important lesson taught in a story

6. Which of the following would you include in a report?

    A a description of imaginary characters

    B sentences that end with rhyming words

    C an outline of a story's plot

    D a main idea and supporting details

7. Which prefix do you add to the word *approve* to create a new word that means "to not approve"?

    A *non-*

    B *dis-*

    C *un-*

    D *in-*

8. Read this passage from "Thank You, Lewis and Clark!"

> Traveling upstream was slower than going downstream. But that was how the Shaws liked it. They thought it was worth the extra effort and time in order to really see everything the river had to offer. This section of the Missouri was part of the National Wild and Scenic River trail. That meant it was part of the original route followed by the explorers Lewis and Clark. It was also the longest stretch of unspoiled land along the Missouri. There was a lot to see.

In what way is the Shaw family like Lewis and Clark?

    A Both the Shaw family and Lewis and Clark traveled through a desert.

    B The Shaw family and Lewis and Clark traveled at the same time.

    C Both the Shaw family and Lewis and Clark explored a river.

    D Both the Shaw family and Lewis and Clark were on vacation.

9. What is the best way to rewrite the sentence below?

> what is the fastest way to get too mulberry street.

    A What is the fastest way to get too Mulberry street?

    B what is the fastest way to get to Mulberry Street.

    C What is the fastest way to get to Mulberry Street?

    D What is the fastest way to get to mulberry street!

10. Read these lines from the song "Cumberland Gap."

> Me and my wife and my wife's pap,
> We're all going down to Cumberland Gap
> *Chorus:*
> Cumberland Gap, Cumberland Gap.
> Hey! [Escape] down yonder to Cumberland Gap.

What does the Cumberland Gap symbolize in these lines from the song?

A a duty to remain at home with your family

B a desire to spend time by yourself

C a terrible danger that should be avoided

D a chance to get away

11. Which prefix do you add to the word *afraid* to create a new word that means "not afraid"?

A *un-*

B *non-*

C *in-*

D *dis-*

12. Read this passage from "The Life and Travels of Jedediah Smith."

> We made it to the Sierra Nevada by May. It was cold up in those mountains at night! Then we struggled through the harsh Nevada desert on our way back to Utah. In July 1827, we returned to the Great Salt Lake, the exact spot we had started the year before.

By reading on, you can figure out that the Sierra Nevada is a —

A type of lake

B group of mountains

C large desert

D famous salt mine

13. Which prefix do you add to the word *complete* to create a new word that means "not complete"?

A *non-*

B *in-*

C *dis-*

D *un-*

Read this passage from "Thank You, Lewis and Clark!" Answer questions 14 and 15.

> One of Sacagawea's <u>contributions</u> was her knowledge of native plants. She knew how to identify them, where to find them, and how to prepare them. These plants added much-needed variety to the group's diet.
>
> After hearing about the plant gathering, Diane had been excited to find a wild licorice plant at one of the stops. It was one of the plants Sacagawea collected. Diane took a picture of the plant. "Thank you!" she exclaimed.

14. What does the word <u>contributions</u> mean in this passage?

   A types of plants found in the wilderness
   B things people can eat
   C ways someone helps a group
   D methods of gathering plants

15. In what way is Diane like Sacagawea?

   A She knows what a wild licorice plant looks like.
   B She cooks wild licorice plants for the group.
   C She likes the taste of licorice.
   D She doesn't know anything about native plants.

Read this passage from "From Sea to Shining Sea." Answer questions 16 and 17.

> In the early 1800s, the land between the Mississippi River and the Pacific coast was untamed. Native Americans had lived there for thousands of years, but they did not believe in owning land. The U.S. government did. And so did the American people. The country wanted to grow, and that growth required land.

16. In this passage, what does land symbolize to the American people?

   A traveling   C friendship
   B growth   D danger

17. Based on the passage, how were government and Native American views of owning land similar or different?

   A The U.S. government wanted to buy land, but the Native Americans would not sell the land they owned.
   B Both the U.S. government and Native Americans wanted to own more land.
   C Native Americans did not believe in owning land, but the U.S. government did.
   D Both felt that growth required owning more land near the Mississippi River.

Choose the word that best completes each sentence for questions 18 and 19.

18. An instrument for showing direction is called _____.

    A a compass   **C** a caravan

    B a companion   **D** an atlas

19. A noisy rushing about or disturbance is known as a _____.

    A colonization   **C** companion

    B commotion   **D** caravan

Read this passage from "The Life and Travels of Jedediah Smith." Answer questions 20 and 21.

> We kept going until we got to the Mojave Desert. We were starving and parched from thirst. The hot wind blew nonstop. Our horses died and we had to walk for miles. The kindness of the folks at the mission of San Gabriel saved us from an insufferable fate.
>
> Beaver trapping was good along the California coast. My men and I could have stayed on there and been happy. But the Mexican government wouldn't let us trade there. So we packed up and traveled north through the Central Valley of California.

20. In what way are the people at the San Gabriel mission different from the Mexican government?

    A The people at the San Gabriel mission were in California, and the Mexican government was in the Mojave Desert.

    B The people at the San Gabriel mission wanted the trappers to leave, but the Mexican government wanted the trappers to stay.

    C The people at the San Gabriel mission welcomed the trappers, but the Mexican government did not want the trappers around.

    D The people at the San Gabriel mission wanted the trappers to give them money, and the Mexican government wanted to pay the trappers.

21. By breaking the word *insufferable* into parts, you can figure out that it means —

    A free from suffering

    B able to survive

    C very easy to deal with

    D too difficult to bear

Read this passage from "Thank You, Lewis and Clark!" Answer questions 22 and 23.

> She told the family that in 1803, President Jefferson had asked Meriwether Lewis to map the Missouri River. Lewis had formed a group known as the Corps of Discovery. William Clark helped lead the group. The group included skilled boatmen. Along the way they were joined by a French interpreter and his Native American wife, Sacagawea. Sacagawea's baby made the trip. So did Lewis's dog. The group did not have an <u>atlas</u> to guide the way. They were traveling in uncharted lands. What an adventure!

22. Based on the passage, what did Lewis and Clark have in common?

    A Both brought their dogs along for the trip on the Missouri River.
    B Both were French interpreters who formed a discovery group.
    C Both traveled with President Jefferson on the Missouri River.
    D Both were adventurers who explored new lands.

23. What does the word <u>atlas</u> mean in this passage?

    A a long river
    B an experienced leader
    C a book of maps
    D a person who speaks two languages

Read this passage. The sentences are numbered. Answer questions 24 and 25.

> (1) Kadin's mother was always reminding him to take his house key with him when he went out to play. (2) "If I'm not home and you don't have _____ key, you won't be able to get inside," she warned him. (3) Sure enough, when Kadin went out on Saturday afternoon, _____ forgot to take the key with him. (4) When he got home, he had to sit on the front steps until his mother returned from the store. (5) Kadin never forgot his key again.

24. Which word best completes sentence 2?

    A her   **C** their
    B your   **D** his

25. Which word best completes sentence 3?

    A it   **C** him
    B she   **D** he

Student _____ Date _____

Student Theme Progress Test Record

Skills Tested	Item Numbers (cross out numbers for items answered incorrectly)	Student Score	Criterion Score	If the student scored less than the Criterion Score, use these Reteaching Tools:
Comprehension Make Connections: Compare/Contrast Information	2 8 15 17 20 22	____ of 6	5 / 6	**Make Connections: Compare/Contrast Information:** Comprehension Bridge 9
Use Fix-Up Strategies	12 21	____ of 2	1 / 2	**Use Fix-Up Strategies:** Comprehension Bridge 8
Target Skill Understand Symbolism	5 10 16	____ of 3	2 / 3	**Understand Symbolism:** Teacher's Guide p. 290
Vocabulary	14 18 19 23	____ of 4	3 / 4	**Vocabulary:** During independent reading time, review student's Vocabulary Journal and discuss how to improve the journal entries
Word Study Prefix *un-*	1 11	____ of 2	1 / 2	**Prefix *un-*:** Sourcebook p. 269 Teacher's Guide p. 272
Prefixes *non-*, *in-*, and *dis-*	4 7 13	____ of 3	2 / 3	**Prefixes *non-*, *in-*, and *dis-*:** Sourcebook p. 281 Teacher's Guide p. 288
Writing: Process Writing Process: Editing	3 9	____ of 2	1 / 2	**Process: Editing** Writing Bridge 17
Form: Report	6	____ of 1	1 / 1	**Form: Report:** Writing Bridge 18
Writing: Grammar Subject and Object Pronouns	25	____ of 1	1 / 1	**Subject and Object Pronouns:** Writing Resource Guide p. 17 Writer's Handbook p. 22
Possessive Pronouns	24	____ of 1	1 / 1	**Possessive Pronouns:** Writing Resource Guide p. 18 Writer's Handbook p. 22
		____ / 25	18 / 25	

Answer Key

1. D   2. B   3. A   4. C   5. A   6. D   7. B   8. C   9. C   10. D   11. A   12. B   13. B

14. C   15. A   16. B   17. C   18. A   19. B   20. C   21. D   22. D   23. C   24. B   25. D

THEME ⑩ Ongoing Test Practice

SAMPLE
Read the passage. Then answer the question.

Michelle Jefferson is running for mayor. She has lived in this city all her life. She is married to Richard Jefferson, and they have three young children. Michelle Jefferson will bring jobs to our city and make our streets safer. Please support her on Election Day.

S. What is the main purpose of this passage?

   A to describe Michelle Jefferson's family
   B to convince you to vote for Michelle Jefferson
   C to let you know when Election Day is
   D to explain how Michelle Jefferson will bring jobs to the city

---

Read the passage. Then read each question. Circle the letter of the correct answer.

Kit Carson

Christopher "Kit" Carson was born on December 24, 1809, in Madison County, Kentucky. A short time later, his family moved to Missouri. When Kit was about nine years old, his father died. To help make money for the family, Kit got a job working for a saddle maker on the Santa Fe Trail.

While working on the trail, Kit met a lot of people who were heading west. Kit was fascinated by the stories people told about what they would see out west. He spent countless days watching the wagon trains pass until 1826, when he ran away in search of adventure.

Over the next 14 years, Kit explored the West. He became known as a skilled trapper and guide. In 1843 he was hired by a <u>pioneer</u> named John Fremont. Together they traveled through the Rocky Mountains and into Oregon and California. They mapped trails to the Pacific Ocean, which were later used by many people who went west.

When Fremont returned home, he wrote many stories about Kit's adventures. The stories were popular among people of all ages. Children in particular couldn't get enough of the Kit Carson tales. The stories told of a man who was as strong as an ox and as brave as a lion. Before long, Kit Carson was larger than life. When the Mexican-American War broke out in 1846, Kit worked for the United States. He helped relay messages through dangerous territory. He also fought alongside the soldiers, often leading them in battle.

A few years later, the Civil War began and Kit was called back to duty. He helped organize the First New Mexico Volunteer Infantry and successfully fought off the Confederate army. Thanks in large part to his efforts, New Mexico remained part of the Union. After the war ended, Kit retired and became a rancher. He died in Fort Lyons, Colorado, in 1868.

1. Read this sentence from the passage.

> Kit was fascinated by the stories people told about what they would see out west.

The author included this sentence in the passage to describe —

A how Kit Carson became famous
B why Kit Carson decided to go west
C Kit Carson's role in the Civil War
D where young Kit Carson worked

2. Which sentence from the passage includes an exaggeration?

A *Before long, Kit Carson was a very famous man.*
B *He also fought alongside the soldiers, often leading them in battle.*
C *He became known as a skilled trapper and guide.*
D *They told of a man who was as strong as an ox and as brave as a lion.*

3. In this passage, a <u>pioneer</u> is a person who —

A opens the way for others to follow
B makes maps for a living
C fights in a war
D climbs very large mountains

4. Which sentence from the passage includes exaggeration?

A *Kit was fascinated by the stories people told about what they would see out west.*
B *After the war ended, Kit retired and became a rancher.*
C *Before long, Kit Carson was larger than life.*
D *Thanks in large part to his efforts, New Mexico remained part of the Union.*

5. Read this sentence from the passage.

> A few years later, the Civil War began and Kit was called back to duty.

The author included this sentence in the passage to —

A describe Kit Carson's role during the Civil War
B show how the government convinced Kit to help fight the war
C explain why Kit Carson decided to fight in the Civil War
D show that the government still considered Kit an important leader

Answer the following question on a separate sheet of paper.

6. Why did the author include information about John Fremont in this passage?

THEME ⑩ Theme Progress Test

Read each question. Fill in the correct circle on your answer document.

1. Which prefix do you add to the word *examine* to make a new word that means "examine again"?

   A *pre-*   **C** *non-*

   B *re-*   **D** *dis-*

2. Read these lines about the railroad from the poem "King of the West."

   > New towns spring up
   > as we pass each station.
   > Where once were grass and buffalo,
   > are now farms and shops,
   > thundering west—all the way to the setting sun.

   How has the land changed as a result of the railroad?

   A There are more buffalo now.

   B There are fewer people now.

   C There are more stores now.

   D There are fewer farms now.

3. Which of the following best completes the sentence below?

   > "Don't worry," he said. "_____ let you know when we plan to arrive."

   A Well

   B Well'

   C Wel'l

   D We'll

4. What does the word <u>ascend</u> mean in the sentence below?

   > The firefighter had to <u>ascend</u> the ladder in order to reach the woman trapped on the second floor of the building.

   A climb up

   B climb down

   C put up

   D take down

5. Making inferences about the author's purpose for writing helps you understand —

    A how to connect ideas in the text
    B ways to develop fix-up strategies
    C why the author wrote the text
    D how to classify information in the text

6. Which of the following sentences includes exaggeration?

    A It feels warm outside, but the sky is cloudy and gray.
    B It's going to take me forever to read this whole book.
    C Bonnie asked Carla if she could borrow one of her sweaters.
    D When do you think Rafael will return from his trip to Spain?

7. Which prefix do you add to the word *view* to make a new word that means "view in advance"?

    A *pre-*
    B *dis-*
    C *un-*
    D *re-*

8. Read this passage from "Land Rush!"

    > Justin woke up before dawn with a start. He heard a wooden spoon rattling in an iron skillet. "Why are we getting up so early, Lucy?" he asked his sister. "It's hardly light!" Justin began to rearrange his bedroll.

    If you wanted to write a story similar to this one, how would you organize your story?

    A by cause and effect
    B from problem to solution
    C from strongest argument to weakest argument
    D in the order that events occurred

9. What is the correct way to write the words *they are* as a contraction?

    A their
    B there
    C the're
    D they're

10. Read this passage about the Pony Express from "One Hundred Sixty Miles of Bad Weather!"

> As people settled the West, they needed to communicate with those in the East. Mail was the only way to get news back and forth. But there were few mail carriers, and the system was slow. In 1860, some businessmen organized a relay system of horses and riders to deliver mail. They traveled across the country in just ten days.

What was the author's purpose for writing this passage?

A to tell the story of a famous Pony Express rider

B to explain why the Pony Express was started

C to explain why modern mail is faster than the Pony Express

D to tell how much it cost to send a letter by Pony Express

11. Which of the following sentences includes exaggeration?

A Paula is the fastest runner on the track team.

B Paula set three school records last season.

C Paula is as fast as lightning.

D Many people are looking forward to watching Paula race this season.

12. Read this passage from "Catherine Haun's Journey Across the Plains, 1849."

> The Gold Rush of 1849 drew a quarter of a million people to Northern California. Some people were seeking adventure. Many were escaping debt. They hoped to strike it rich and rebuild their lives. Catherine Haun and her husband were among this latter group.

The author wrote this passage to —

A explain different reasons why people went to California in 1849

B describe the town where Catherine Haun grew up

C identify some famous people who went to California in 1849

D explain what the Gold Rush of 1849 was

13. Which word best completes the sentence below?

> The neighbors said that _____ been planning a trip to the beach this weekend.

A they   **C** they've

B they'll   **D** they're

Read this passage from "Land Rush!" Answer questions 14 and 15.

> Justin thought about the thousands of people eagerly waiting with them at the borders of Oklahoma Territory. At noon today, April 22, 1889, everyone would make a frantic dash into the territory to claim free land. Justin wondered how many other families needed a new home in Oklahoma as desperately as his family did.
>
> "Where do you reckon we'll end up?" Justin asked Ma.
>
> "I'm headed for Guthrie," Ma said. "Meet me there. A widow can make a decent living in a town. And I have you and Lucy to help me."

14. What is the function of the dialogue in this passage?

   A   to describe the setting
   B   to explain where Justin's family is from
   C   to describe how many people were waiting at the border
   D   to advance the plot of the story

15. In what way are the people waiting at the border alike?

   A   They are all widows.
   B   They all want free land.
   C   They are all from Oklahoma.
   D   They are all headed for Guthrie.

Read this passage. The sentences are numbered. Answer questions 16 and 17.

> (1) Stories about Paul Bunyan are a lot of fun, even though _____ are obviously not true. (2) People say that Paul Bunyan and his blue ox, Babe, were so large that _____ footsteps created all the lakes in Minnesota.

16. Which word best completes sentence 1?

   A   it
   B   them
   C   their
   D   they

17. Which word best completes sentence 2?

   A   their
   B   its
   C   those
   D   his

Choose the word that best completes each sentence for questions 18 and 19.

18. When you _____, you trade goods or services for other goods or services.

    A   ascend

    B   inspect

    C   barter

    D   pioneer

19. The house, buildings, and land where a family lives are called _____.

    A   an expansion

    B   a migration

    C   an existence

    D   a homestead

Read these lines from the poem "King of the West." Answer questions 20 and 21.

> Here we come,
> a million tons of iron and steel,
> powered by coal and steam,
> stronger than countless horses,
> faster than a shooting star,
> thundering west—all the way to the setting sun.
>
> The locomotive
> is King of the West
> The leader of all
> that is to come,
> thundering west—all the way to the setting sun.

20. Why does the author use the phrase "thundering west" in this passage?

    A   to tell the reader that the locomotive travels fastest in the rain

    B   to show that the locomotive moves with great force and noise

    C   to explain why the locomotive is traveling westward

    D   to help the reader understand why the locomotive is called the King of the West

21. What does the word locomotive mean in this passage?

    A   an engine used to push or pull railroad cars

    B   a very strong horse

    C   the leader of a town in the Old West

    D   a machine used to make steel

Read this passage from "Catherine Haun's Journey Across the Plains, 1849." Answer questions 22 and 23.

We finally reached Sacramento, California, on November 4, 1849. . . . There were only a half dozen houses, all at very high prices. My husband resorted to drawing up a will and charging $150.00. This seemed to be a lucky sign. We gave up all thought of hunting for gold, and he hung out a sign as a lawyer. After 2,400 miles and nine months of living in a tent, we were glad to settle down. We prepared for our new life.

22. The author most likely wrote this passage to —

   A explain the difference between a gold miner and a lawyer
   B identify the different people that made the journey with the narrator
   C explain what happened at the end of the narrator's journey
   D describe what the narrator's journey to California was like

23. Which word best replaces *gave up* in line 4 of this passage?

   A abandoned
   B donated
   C quit
   D stopped

Read this passage from "One Hundred Sixty Miles of Bad Weather!" Answer questions 24 and 25.

Once a rider started out, he couldn't stop until he got the mail to the next station. If there was no rider to replace him there, then he had to ride on. Every Pony Express rider understood these things very clearly. No matter the weather, no matter what happened along the route, the mail had to go through.

24. The author wrote this passage to —

   A describe the different types of Pony Express riders
   B explain the duties of a Pony Express rider
   C identify the people who worked for the Pony Express
   D explain where the Pony Express stations were located

25. Which word could best replace the word *ride* in this passage?

   A walk   C continue
   B try   D rest

Student _____ Date _____

THEME 10

Student Theme Progress Test Record

Skills Tested	Item Numbers (cross out numbers for items answered incorrectly)	Student Score	Criterion Score	If the student scored less than the Criterion Score, use these Reteaching Tools:
Comprehension Infer: Author's Purpose	5 10 12 20 22 24	____ of 6	5 / 6	**Infer: Author's Purpose:** Comprehension Bridge 10
Make Connections: Compare/Contrast Information	2 15	____ of 2	1 / 2	**Make Connections: Compare/Contrast Information:** Comprehension Bridge 9
Target Skill Understand Dialogue	14	____ of 1	1 / 1	**Understand Dialogue:** Teacher's Guide p. 313
Understand Exaggeration and Hyperbole	6 11	____ of 2	1 / 2	**Understand Exaggeration and Hyperbole:** Teacher's Guide p. 322
Vocabulary	4 18 19 21	____ of 4	3 / 4	**Vocabulary:** During independent reading time, review student's Vocabulary Journal and discuss how to improve the journal entries
Word Study Prefixes *re-* and *pre-*	1 7	____ of 2	1 / 2	**Prefixes *re-* and *pre-*:** Sourcebook p. 299 Teacher's Guide p. 304
Contractions	3 9 13	____ of 3	2 / 3	**Contractions:** Sourcebook p. 311 Teacher's Guide p. 320
Writing: Process Writing Trait: Word Choice	23 25	____ of 2	1 / 2	**Trait: Word Choice:** Writing Bridge 19
Organizational Pattern: Sequence	8	____ of 1	1 / 1	**Organizational Pattern: Sequence:** Writing Bridge 20
Writing: Grammar Singular and Plural Pronouns	16	____ of 1	1 / 1	**Singular and Plural Pronouns:** Writing Resource Guide p. 19 Writer's Handbook p. 22
Pronouns	17	____ of 1	1 / 1	**Pronouns:** Writing Resource Guide p. 20 Writer's Handbook p. 22
		____ / 25	**18 / 25**	

Answer Key

1. B   2. C   3. D   4. A   5. C   6. B   7. A   8. D   9. D   10. B   11. C   12. A   13. C

14. D   15. B   16. D   17. A   18. C   19. D   20. B   21. A   22. C   23. A   24. B   25. C

THEME ⑪ Ongoing Test Practice

SAMPLE
Read the passage. Then answer the question.

The *Mona Lisa* is one of the most famous paintings in the world. It shows a woman sitting with her hands together. Some people believe that the woman is smiling, while others argue she is not. Either way, the *Mona Lisa* is a very beautiful painting.

S. If you looked at the *Mona Lisa*, what question might you ask to decide whether the woman is smiling?

   A Why is the painting famous?
   B What year was the painting completed?
   C Does the woman seem happy?
   D How is the woman wearing her hair?

Read the passage. Then read each question. Circle the letter of the correct answer.

The Legend of John Henry

One day ol' John Henry decided it was time to get a job. He heard that the railroads were going to be extended all the way to the Pacific Ocean and that strong men were needed to lay the track. Ol' John Henry was the tallest, strongest man for miles around, so this was the perfect job for him. He went down to the railroad office and told the boss man, "Go get me one of those big nine-pound hammers, and I'll drive those steel stakes into the ground faster than ten men!"

That's how John Henry became a steel-driving man. He drove stakes into the ground as fast as can be. Other men had to hammer their stakes a dozen times, but not ol' John Henry. He'd just hit it once, and *BAM!* it was in the ground.

Even with John Henry on the team, laying railroad tracks was a long, difficult job. It took a lot of workers, and it cost a lot of money to pay and feed so many people. So the boss man decided to fire the workers and replace them with a machine that could pound the stakes into the ground automatically. Of course, ol' John Henry didn't like the sound of that, so he challenged the machine to a race, telling the boss man, "If I win, we all get to keep our jobs. If that machine wins, we'll gladly quit."

The boss man knew the offer was too good to <u>resist</u>, and soon the race was on. Once the machine was fired up, it went off like a flash, hammering away at those spikes so fast it'd make your head spin. Well, ol' John Henry got fired up, too, and he started hammering like he'd never done before. They both moved so quickly that soon they were out of sight, laying track all across the country.

They worked until they could work no more. In the end, that machine broke down and fell apart just before ol' John Henry slammed down his last stake. But it was too much for him, too. The poor man fell to the ground, and just before he closed his eyes for the last time, he whispered, "We win."

1. The illustration helps show —

   A where John Henry's hammer was made
   B why John Henry raced the machine
   C how hard John Henry worked
   D in which direction John Henry was moving

2. What does the word <u>resist</u> mean in this story?

   A refuse
   B consider
   C describe
   D reply

3. The onlookers in the illustration probably thought John Henry was —

   A strange
   B uninteresting
   C funny
   D impressive

4. Based on the illustration, you can guess that John Henry was —

   A determined
   B afraid
   C miserable
   D carefree

5. Why does the author repeat the name "ol' John Henry"?

   A to remind you who is telling the story
   B to focus your attention on the main character
   C to make you believe that John Henry was very old
   D to describe how other people saw John Henry

Answer the following question on a separate sheet of paper.

6. Based on the illustration and information from the passage, how can you compare or contrast John Henry and the machine?

Name _____ Date _____

THEME **11** Theme Progress Test

Read each question. Fill in the correct circle on your answer document.

1. Which list of words contains all pronouns?

   A you, me, them
   B large, smooth, green
   C deer, uncle, clock
   D dancer, runner, swimmer

2. What is the purpose of writing an observation log?

   A to record interesting details from a story that you read
   B to see how something does or does not change over time
   C to describe different methods of looking at things to the reader
   D to explain the result of an event that you witnessed long ago

3. Asking questions about visuals that accompany a text helps you —

   A determine which visuals are not important
   B explain the author's purpose for writing the text
   C determine the title of the text
   D better understand how images relate to the text

4. What is the correct way to abbreviate the word *versus*?

   A vs.   **C** vss.
   B vrs.   **D** vers.

5. Which strategy helps you make sure that your writing flows well?

   A making all your sentences the same length
   B reading your writing aloud to see if it sounds good
   C structuring all your sentences the same way
   D repeating the same ideas over and over again

6. A writer repeats words and ideas in a poem to —

   A help you figure out when the poem was written
   B draw your attention away from the meaning of the poem
   C focus your attention on important themes and concepts
   D help you remember who wrote the poem

7. What is the correct way to abbreviate the word *December*?

   A Dec.

   B Dece.

   C Dmb.

   D Dr.

8. Which words in the sentence below are pronouns?

> My friend Steven asked if I wanted to go to the movies with him on Friday.

   A asked, wanted, go

   B Steven, movies, Friday

   C to, with, on

   D My, I, him

9. Which of the following would you include in an observation log?

   A a greeting to the reader

   B a description of what you saw

   C a list of hobbies you enjoy

   D a description of the characters in a story

10. What is the correct abbreviation for the word *gallon*?

   A gal   **C** gon

   B gln   **D** glln

11. Read this passage from "What Comes Down."

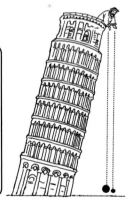

> Mrs. Estes started our gravity lesson with a question. "If Galileo dropped weights of 8 lb and 15 lb off the Leaning Tower of Pisa, which would hit the ground first?" Everyone shouted that the heavier weight would hit first. Instead of telling us if we were right, Mrs. Estes sent Simon, Claire, and me outside to do experiments.

Based on the illustration that accompanies the passage, what did Galileo's experiment probably show?

   A Objects fall from a leaning tower at an unusual angle.

   B Objects of any weight will drop at the same speed.

   C Dropping weights from a tower causes a tower to lean.

   D Objects fall at different speeds depending on their size.

12. Read this passage from "How Gravity Was Invented."

> But as you know, things on Earth change. Spring changes to summer, tadpoles change into frogs, etc. And so it was on long-ago Earth that things began to change.

The author repeats the word *change* in this passage to —

A make the reader think about the different seasons

B show how Earth is different than it was long ago

C draw the reader's attention to an important idea in the story

D help the reader imagine what happens as a tadpole grows into a frog

13. Read this passage from "What Comes Down."

> NASA has conducted one of Galileo's falling-objects experiments on the moon. Galileo claimed that, in the absence of air resistance, a feather and stone would drop at the same rate. What better place to see if he was right than on the moon, where there is no air? *Apollo 15* astronaut David Scott dropped a feather and a hammer.

Based on the visual that accompanies this passage, you can tell that —

A Galileo's claim was incorrect

B Galileo's claim was correct

C the feather hit the ground first

D the hammer hit the ground first

Read this passage. The sentences are numbered. Answer questions 14 and 15.

> (1) Davy Crockett is one of the most famous people to come from Tennessee. (2) He was also one of the _____. (3) Throughout his life, he faced wild animals in the forest and angry enemies on the battlefield. (4) Today Davy Crockett is remembered as a great American hero.

14. Which word best completes sentence 2?

A brave   **C** bravest

B braver   **D** bravely

15. Which word in the passage is used as a proper adjective?

A famous   **C** angry

B Tennessee   **D** American

Read this passage from "An Out-of-This-World Vacation." Answer questions 16 and 17.

> Another company is building a craft that is carried into the air by a "mothership." In this design, the small spaceplane is attached to a larger airplane for takeoff. Once the large plane has reached a high altitude, it will <u>release</u> the spaceplane, which will then rocket into space.

16. From the passage and the diagram, you can tell that the spaceplane separates from the "mothership" and flies into space —

    A as the mothership takes off from the runway
    B when they reach 44,000 feet
    C when they reach 370,000 feet
    D as the mothership lands

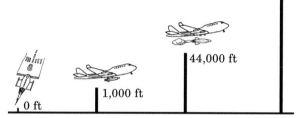

Flight Stages of Spaceplane

17. What does the word <u>release</u> mean in this passage?

    A strengthen
    B carry
    C set free
    D blast off

Choose the word that best completes each sentence for questions 18 and 19.

18. If something is funny, it is _____.

    A elevation
    B brief
    C force
    D comical

19. When an object is dropped, _____ is what makes it fall to the ground.

    A accelerate
    B elevation
    C gravity
    D waver

Read these lines from the poem "Walking in Space." Answer questions 20 and 21.

> Our spacecraft lands on alien land.
> My emotions surge till I almost cry.
> That's when I realize how much I love
> That beautiful blue marble in the sky.
>
> My feet touch ground that is not my own.
> I watch a shooting star zip by.
> I am so far away from home.
> My beautiful blue marble in the sky.

20. The author most likely wrote this poem to —

   A identify the types of objects found in outer space

   B explain how a spacecraft works

   C describe what the surface of the moon looks like

   D express her feelings about Earth

21. Why does the author repeat the phrase "beautiful blue marble in the sky"?

   A to focus your attention on how far the narrator has traveled through space

   B to explain that there are large marbles floating around in space

   C to help you understand the focus of the poem

   D to explain what it's like to land on alien land

Read this passage from "An Out-of-This-World Vacation." Answer questions 22 and 23.

> People involved in space tourism <u>calculate</u> that prices will continue to come down. . . . [Eric] Anderson thinks that everyone will be able to afford space travel in 50 years.

Cost of Space Tourism	
2001	$ 20,000,000
2008	$ 200,000
2021	$ 50,000

22. Based on the passage and chart, you can tell that space travel is becoming —

   A more affordable   **C** more expensive

   B more popular   **D** more dangerous

23. What does the word <u>calculate</u> mean in this passage?

   A save money for a trip into outer space

   B think about reasons people would go into outer space

   C make a guess about the future

   D use math to come up with a number

Read this passage. Answer questions 24 and 25.

In 1687 a man named Isaac Newton published a book about gravity. Newton's idea explained that objects attract one another. His idea also explained why we don't float away from Earth and why Earth and other planets orbit around the sun. Many people say he came up with his great idea when an apple fell from a tree and landed on his head.

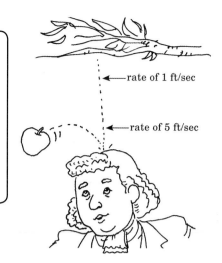

rate of 1 ft/sec

rate of 5 ft/sec

24. Why does the author include the story about an apple falling and hitting Newton on the head?

   A to make the reader laugh
   B to show that complex ideas can come from simple observations
   C to explain where Newton was when he came up with his idea about gravity
   D to show how much Newton liked apples

25. How might the falling apple shown in the illustration have helped Newton come up with his idea?

   A The apple moves faster as it falls, which shows Earth's gravitational pull.
   B The apple slows down as it falls, which shows the sun's gravitational pull.
   C The apple floats, which shows that the Earth has no gravity.
   D The apple's speed stays the same as it falls.

Student _____ Date _____

THEME ⑪

Student Theme Progress Test Record

Skills Tested	Item Numbers (cross out numbers for items answered incorrectly)	Student Score	Criterion Score	If the student scored less than the Criterion Score, use these Reteaching Tools:
Comprehension Ask Questions: Visuals	3 11 13 16 22 25	_____ of 6	5 / 6	**Ask Questions: Visuals:** Comprehension Bridge 11
Infer: Author's Purpose	20 24	_____ of 2	1 / 2	**Infer: Author's Purpose:** Comprehension Bridge 10
Target Skill Identify Repetition of Language	6 12 21	_____ of 3	2 / 3	**Identify Repetition of Language:** Teacher's Guide p. 356
Vocabulary	17 18 19 23	_____ of 4	3 / 4	**Vocabulary:** During independent reading time, review student's Vocabulary Journal and discuss how to improve the journal entries
Word Study Abbreviations	4 7 10	_____ of 3	2 / 3	**Abbreviations:** Sourcebook p. 331 Teacher's Guide p. 338
Writing: Process Writing Trait: Sentence Fluency	5	_____ of 1	1 / 1	**Trait: Sentence Fluency:** Writing Bridge 21
Form: Observation Log	2 9	_____ of 2	1 / 2	**Form: Observation Log:** Writing Bridge 22
Writing: Grammar Adjectives: Comparative and Superlative	14	_____ of 1	1 / 1	**Adjectives: Comparative and Superlative:** Writing Resource Guide p. 22 Writer's Handbook p. 27
Adjectives: Common and Proper	15	_____ of 1	1 / 1	**Adjectives: Common and Proper:** Writing Resource Guide p. 21 Writer's Handbook p. 26
Pronouns	1 8	_____ of 2	1 / 2	**Pronouns:** Writing Resource Guide p. 19 Writer's Handbook p. 22
		_____ / 25	18 / 25	

Answer Key

1. A   2. B   3. D   4. A   5. B   6. C   7. A   8. D   9. B   10. A   11. B   12. C   13. B

14. C   15. D   16. B   17. C   18. D   19. C   20. D   21. C   22. A   23. D   24. B   25. A

THEME **12** Ongoing Test Practice

SAMPLE
Read the passage. Then answer the question.

James didn't get home from school until after 6:30 P.M. He'd been working on a report in the library all afternoon, and he was exhausted. He climbed the 26 steps to his family's apartment and opened the heavy wooden door. After shutting it, he sat down in his favorite chair and fell asleep.

S. Which information in the passage is most important?

  A James is exhausted from working hard on his report.
  B There are 26 steps leading up to James's apartment.
  C The chair James falls asleep on is his favorite.
  D The door to James's apartment is made of heavy wood.

Read the passage. Then read each question. Circle the letter of the correct answer.

The Parachute

What would happen if you jumped out of an airplane? You would likely fall and be badly hurt. But every day, people all over the world jump out of airplanes and float safely to the ground. How do they do it? They use parachutes.

A parachute is a very large piece of cloth with special cords that attach to a person's body. When a parachute opens up as a jumper falls, it stretches out and fills with air. This slows the fall, allowing the jumper to drift down to Earth without harm.

The first <u>attempt</u> at creating a parachute took place in the Middle Ages. In the year AD 852, a man jumped off of a high tower with a large cloak that had sticks in it to keep it open. It was a new idea, but jumping from a tower with a giant kite may not have been the safest experiment. Even though his landing was rough, the man survived the jump.

In the early 1480s, the famous scientist and artist Leonardo da Vinci drew a picture of his idea for a device that would allow a person to fall from a great height safely. His drawing looked very much like a modern parachute, and it inspired others to work with similar ideas.

The first person to successfully test a modern-style parachute was Faust Vrancic. He called his invention "Homo Volans," which means "Flying Man." Like the man with the cloak, he also jumped from a tower. However, he landed without injury. Unfortunately, few people heard about the invention, and it was largely forgotten.

In 1785 a French inventor named Jean-Pierre Blanchard began experimenting with dropping objects and animals from a hot-air balloon using a device called a parachute. In 1793 he used the parachute to save himself when his balloon popped.

Today, parachutes are used mostly by the military and by people who skydive for fun. They are also used to help slow down certain types of race cars as well as airplanes that land on large boats called aircraft carriers. The parachute has gone from being an odd idea to being the basis for an exciting sport and a useful invention that has saved countless lives.

1. What is the most important information about Leonardo da Vinci in paragraph 4?

   A He was a scientist.
   B He was an artist.
   C He drew an early parachute.
   D He lived in the 1400s.

2. What does the word <u>attempt</u> mean in this story?

   A the act of trying
   B the act of succeeding
   C the act of falling
   D the act of building

3. Which detail about Jean-Pierre Blanchard is most important?

   A He flew in a hot-air balloon.
   B He fell from a hot-air balloon and was saved by a parachute.
   C He dropped objects from a hot-air balloon.
   D He was from France.

4. Which of these sentences from the passage is an example of humor?

   A *It was a new idea, but jumping from a tower with a giant kite may not have been the safest experiment.*
   B *His drawing looked very much like a modern parachute.*
   C *The first person to successfully test a modern-style parachute was Faust Vrancic.*
   D *You would likely fall and be badly hurt.*

5. What is the most important information about parachutes in this passage?

   A A parachute is made mostly of cloth.
   B A parachute can help you survive a fall from a great height.
   C Special cords are used to attach a parachute to a person's body.
   D Faust Vrancic called the parachute the "Flying Man."

Answer the following question on a separate sheet of paper.

6. Which details are most important to support the main idea of this passage?

THEME **12** Theme Progress Test

Read each question. Fill in the correct circle on your answer document.

1. Read these lines from the poem "The Cyclists' Song."

   > Their bikes are the lightest
   > Titanium steel
   > Their tires the fastest—
   > Discs (not spokes) in the wheels

   The author uses rhythm in this poem to —

   A describe a character
   B set the mood of the poem
   C identify a point of view
   D focus your attention on the parts of a bike

2. When you rank information from a passage, you —

   A use the information to create images in your mind
   B think about ways to use new information
   C connect the information to what you already know
   D decide how important the information is

3. If you organize events in sequence when you write, you —

   A put events in the order that they happen
   B put events in order of importance
   C order details from most interesting to least interesting
   D order details from least interesting to most interesting

4. Read this passage from "Extreme Dogboarding."

   > Chay felt like a million dollars. He put down his skateboard, and he and
   > Megan headed for the water fountain.

   What does the author mean when she writes that "Chay felt like a million dollars"?

   A Chay felt really great.
   B Chay felt very rich.
   C Chay felt unhappy.
   D Chay felt thirsty.

5. Read this passage from "Famous Firsts."

> Bannister thought another key was training. He believed that by slow, steady training he could improve his running time by two or three seconds each year. Bannister trained only 45 minutes a day. Most runners trained two to three hours a day.

Which information in this passage is most important?

A Bannister trained to improve his running time.

B Bannister trained for less than an hour a day.

C Most other runners trained for a few hours each day.

D Bannister believed slow, steady training was the key to improvement.

6. What does the word <u>courageous</u> mean in the sentence below?

> The <u>courageous</u> police officer ran into the burning building to help.

A skilled

B brave

C cautious

D frightened

7. Read this passage from "Manny Masters Curling."

> Manny looked toward Pablo, the team's lead, standing inside the hog line at the other end of the rink. That line was the minimum distance Manny had to move the stone. On either side, Mark and Josh stood with brooms in hand, ready to sweep if needed.

Which detail from the passage is most important?

A Mark and Josh are holding brooms.

B Pablo is the leader of the team.

C Pablo is standing inside the hog line.

D Manny must move the stone to the hog line.

8. When you are ready to publish your writing, you —

A put your topic ideas into a graphic organizer

B make a clean copy of your writing and share it with others

C review your writing for punctuation, spelling, and capitalization errors

D revise your writing by adding and removing details

9. Which words in the sentence below are adverbs?

> Omar did well on his science test because he dutifully studied hard all week.

A did, because, studied

B his, he, all

C well, dutifully, hard

D Omar, test, week

10. Read this passage from "Famous Firsts."

> Then, partway up the mountain, an avalanche buried the climbers' camp. Once everyone was accounted for, Tabei pressed on, playing it by ear. The bruised team inched its way to the top, sometimes crawling on hands and knees. Tabei reached the top on May 16, 1975.

Which of the following visuals would best help you understand how difficult Tabei's journey was after the avalanche?

A a map showing how far the buried camp was from the top of the mountain

B a photograph of Tabei in her hiking gear before she started climbing

C a chart listing the average yearly snowfall on the mountain

D a diagram of the climbers' camp before it was hit by the avalanche

11. Which list of words contains all adverbs?

A thoughtful, careful, boastful

B table, cart, doorway

C slowly, never, happily

D scribble, drink, study

12. Read this passage from "Extreme Dogboarding."

> Just then Chulo [the dog] let out a loud yelp. Megan and Chay spun around just in time to witness Chulo leaping onto the back of Chay's skateboard. Seconds later, the front of the skateboard arced into the air. A startled Chulo and the skateboard flew over a ramp, bit the dust, and landed safely.

Which event from the passage is meant to make the reader laugh?

A Chulo yelping

B Chulo skateboarding

C Megan and Chay watching Chulo

D Chulo landing safely

13. Which list of words contains all adverbs?

   A cardboard, flag, berry

   B drag, push, tear

   C lucky, friendly, sour

   D honestly, joyfully, instantly

Read these lines from "Famous Firsts." Answer questions 14 and 15.

> Kristi put her best foot forward and earned a place on the 1992 U.S. Olympic team. During the competition, Dorothy Hamill stopped by. She wished Kristi luck. With Dorothy's words ringing in her ears, Kristi took to the ice. Her skating earned her a gold medal. She became the first Asian American woman to win Olympic gold in any sport.

14. Which information in this passage is interesting but not important?

   A Kristi met Dorothy Hamill during the competition.

   B Kristi earned a gold medal for her ice skating.

   C Kristi earned a place on the 1992 U.S. Olympic team.

   D Kristi was the first Asian American woman to win a gold medal.

15. How is the information in this passage organized?

   A from most important to least important

   B from least important to most important

   C in sequence

   D by cause and effect

Choose the word that best completes each sentence for questions 16 and 17.

16. A result or an affect can also be called _____.

   A an attempt

   B a physical

   C a consequence

   D a movement

17. A skill or talent can also be called _____.

   A an ability

   B a reaction

   C an attempt

   D a friction

Read this passage from "Extreme Dogboarding." Answer questions 18 and 19.

> Chay watched intently as Megan's back foot smacked the rear end of the skateboard against the concrete while her front foot pulled the skateboard up into the air. When it was Chay's turn, he flipped the skateboard completely over. The second time Chay's foot hit the back end of the skateboard so hard he lost his balance and toppled to the ground. By the fourth try, Chay's move was perfection.
>
> "See, I told you—it's like falling off a log. You're a natural," exclaimed Megan, looking truly impressed.

18. Which of the following details from the passage is most important?

   A Chay watches Megan easily perform the move.
   B Chay is not able to perform the move the first time.
   C On his second try, Chay falls down on the ground.
   D With practice, Chay is able to perform the move.

19. What does the expression "it's like falling off a log" mean?

   A It's a lot of fun.
   B It's very easy.
   C It's dangerous.
   D It's boring.

Read this passage. The sentences are numbered. Answer questions 20 and 21.

> (1) There once lived a famous pirate named Edward Teach. (2) Most people know him better as Blackbeard. (3) Blackbeard was polite and orderly, but he was still considered dangerous.

20. Which word in sentence 1 is an article?

   A once   **C** pirate
   B a   **D** named

21. Which word in sentence 3 is NOT an adjective?

   A polite   **C** considered
   B orderly   **D** dangerous

Read this passage from "Manny Masters Curling." Answer questions 22 and 23.

Manny was about to deliver his team's eighth and final stone.

Manny again focused on Pablo across the rink. As the team captain, it was Pablo's job to tell Manny where to aim the stone. Pablo studied the 15 granite stones that had already been delivered. There were eight from the opponent and seven from their team. Pablo finally decided what Manny needed to do.

22. Which information from the passage is most important?

   A Pablo is the team captain.

   B Manny is focused on Pablo.

   C There are 15 granite stones on the ice.

   D Pablo is trying to help Manny place his team's final stone.

23. Which of the following visuals would best help you understand how Pablo makes his decision?

   A a diagram showing where the other 15 stones are located on the ice

   B a chart showing the average speeds of a curler's throws

   C a photograph of a curling champion

   D a photograph of Manny, Pablo, and their teammates

Read these lines from the poem "The Cyclists' Song." Answer questions 24 and 25.

Their clothing hugs
Like second skins
The starter's gun cracks
And the <u>movement</u> begins.

24. The author uses rhyme in this poem to —

   A make the poem sound pleasing

   B make you focus on the rhyming words

   C make the poem difficult to remember

   D make an important point about cycling

25. What does the word <u>movement</u> mean in this poem?

   A the act of going faster

   B the act of stopping

   C the act of getting going

   D the act of going slower

Student _____ Date _____

THEME 12

Student Theme Progress Test Record

Skills Tested	Item Numbers (cross out numbers for items answered incorrectly)	Student Score	Criterion Score	If the student scored less than the Criterion Score, use these Reteaching Tools:
Comprehension Determine Importance: Rank Information	2 5 7 14 18 22	_____ of 6	5 / 6	**Determine Importance: Rank Information:** Comprehension Bridge 12
Ask Questions: Visuals	10 23	_____ of 2	1 / 2	**Ask Questions: Visuals:** Comprehension Bridge 11
Target Skill Understand Humor	12	_____ of 1	1 / 1	**Understand Humor:** Teacher's Guide p. 379
Recognize Rhythm and Rhyme	1 24	_____ of 2	1 / 2	**Recognize Rhythm and Rhyme:** Teacher's Guide p. 388
Vocabulary	6 16 17 25	_____ of 4	3 / 4	**Vocabulary:** During independent reading time, review student's Vocabulary Journal and discuss how to improve the journal entries
Word Study Idioms	4 19	_____ of 2	1 / 2	**Idioms:** Sourcebook p. 361 Teacher's Guide p. 370
Writing: Process Writing Process: Publishing	8	_____ of 1	1 / 1	**Process: Publishing:** Writing Bridge 23
Organizational Pattern: Sequence	3 15	_____ of 2	1 / 2	**Organizational Pattern: Sequence:** Writing Bridge 24
Writing: Grammar Adverbs	9 11 13	_____ of 3	2 / 3	**Adverbs:** Writing Resource Guide p. 25 Writer's Handbook p. 27
Articles	20	_____ of 1	1 / 1	**Articles:** Writing Resource Guide p. 23 Writer's Handbook p. 26
Review Adjectives	21	_____ of 1	1 / 1	**Adjectives:** Writing Resource Guide p. 24 Writer's Handbook p. 26
		_____ / 25	18 / 25	

Answer Key

1. B   2. D   3. A   4. A   5. D   6. B   7. D   8. B   9. C   10. A   11. C   12. B   13. D

14. A   15. C   16. C   17. A   18. D   19. B   20. B   21. C   22. D   23. A   24. A   25. C

Name _____ Date _____

THEME ⑬ Ongoing Test Practice

SAMPLE
Read the passage. Then answer the question.

A properly made bed helps make a bedroom appear organized. First tug each corner of the fitted sheet tightly on the mattress. Next arrange the flat sheet or blanket on the bed and tuck in the bottom to prevent slipping. Repeat this process for the remaining covers.

S. Why is it a good idea to make your bed?

   A A properly made bed makes a bedroom look organized.
   B Start by tugging the corners of the fitted sheet.
   C Arrange the flat sheet or blanket after tightening the fitted sheet.
   D Arrange the rest of the covers the same way.

Read the passage. Then read each question. Circle the letter of the correct answer.

All the Way to the Moon?

Juanita spent the whole afternoon practicing her swing at the batting cages. Her baseball team had a championship game coming up the next day. She was determined to hit a home run. "All right, I think that's enough for today," her father said. "If you don't give your arms some rest, you'll be too sore to play tomorrow."

At dinner that night, the whole family ate a traditional Colombian meal. As they ate, they talked about the next day's baseball game. "I think I'm going to hit a home run tomorrow," Juanita stated confidently.

"You sure will!" her little brother, Alberto, said. "I bet you'll hit it so high that nobody will know where it went. Maybe you'll even hit it to the moon!"

Everyone laughed at the boy's enthusiasm. "I can <u>assure</u> you that I won't hit the ball to the moon," Juanita replied. "But I'll do my best to knock it over the fence."

When Juanita climbed into bed that night, her eyelids seemed as heavy as concrete. The moment her head hit the pillow, she was fast asleep.

"Time for the big game!" Juanita opened her eyes and sat up. Her father was opening the curtains, filling the room with light. "Let's go, slugger!"

Juanita jumped out of bed and got dressed. Soon they were at the baseball field, and it was Juanita's turn to bat. As she approached home plate, her brother shouted, "Hit it to the moon!"

The pitcher hurled the ball and Juanita swung. CRACK! The ball sailed high into the sky. Everybody watched as it flew out of sight. All of the people were confused, asking where the ball could have gone. Then Juanita heard a news report on a nearby radio. "NASA has just reported that one of its satellites was hit by a baseball. It seemed to be headed for the moon!"

Suddenly Juanita sat up. Her heart was racing as she looked around her dark room. She took a deep breath and lay back down. "It was just a dream," she told herself. "I couldn't *really* hit a baseball all the way to the moon . . . could I?"

1. Which of the following best describes a theme of this story?

   A Baseball is an exciting sport.
   B Setting goals is a good way to prepare for competition.
   C It is impossible to hit a baseball to the moon.
   D Family is more important than competing in sports.

2. What does the word <u>assure</u> mean in this passage?

   A hope   C guess
   B wonder   D promise

3. Which detail from the last paragraph is most important if you are trying to determine how Juanita felt when she woke up?

   A Juanita's heart is racing.
   B Juanita realizes it is nighttime.
   C Juanita is still in bed.
   D Juanita takes a deep breath.

4. What probably causes Juanita to dream of hitting a baseball to the moon?

   A a long day of practice at the batting cages
   B hearing on the radio that someone has hit a baseball to the moon
   C the conversation she has with her family at dinner
   D being nervous about the game and unable to fall asleep

5. Which sentence from the passage is most important if you are reading to find out why Juanita left the batting cages?

   A *Her baseball team had a championship game coming up the next day.*
   B *Juanita spent the whole afternoon practicing her swing at the batting cages.*
   C *At dinner that night, the whole family ate a traditional Colombian meal.*
   D *"If you don't give your arms some rest, you'll be too sore to play tomorrow."*

Answer the following question on a separate sheet of paper.

6. Juanita's baseball team has a championship game coming up. Explain whether it is important to understand this detail when reading the story.

THEME 13 Theme Progress Test

Read each question. Fill in the correct circle on your answer document.

1. Which word in the sentence below is a preposition?

   My friend Joon lives right around the corner.

   A friend
   B lives
   C around
   D corner

2. Why is it important to reflect on your purpose for reading?

   A It helps you decide whether a sentence is a fact or an opinion.
   B It helps you figure out what information is important.
   C It helps you make inferences about what you read.
   D It helps you make connections between the text and your own life.

3. If you were writing an essay to persuade people to visit your school's Web site, it would be most important to include —

   A facts and opinions about the benefits of visiting the school's Web site
   B a list of all the people who worked on creating the Web site
   C some examples of other places where the same information can be found
   D a story describing the creation of the Web site

4. Which of the following suffixes means "without"?

   A -ly
   B -less
   C -ful
   D -able

5. Which list of words contains all prepositions?

   A carpet, stake, dresser
   B curious, thoughtful, clean
   C quietly, joyfully, swiftly
   D above, behind, through

6. Which of the following is something you would do if you were in the prewriting process?

   A correct any spelling and punctuation errors
   B add transitions between ideas
   C think about ideas for your topic
   D support your ideas with details

7. Read this passage from "Tracking the Bird Flu."

   > Sam said "Bird flu is another name for *avian influenza*."
   >
   > I suggested that first we should find a detailed definition. Sam needed to know a few specifics before he could decide what to focus on in his report. He sat down at the computer.

   Why does Sam need more information about avian influenza?

   A so he can avoid catching bird flu
   B so he will do well on his research project
   C so he can learn how to use a computer
   D so he can identify birds that have the flu

8. Read this passage from "Cast Your Vote for the Future."

   > The invention of the printing press revolutionized the world. What would we do without books and other printed material? The telegraph let people send messages across the country in an instant, but the telegraph's time has come and gone. The telephone and its little giant cousin—the cell phone—have had a dramatic impact on communications.

   What is the theme of this passage?

   A Many important inventions have helped people communicate.
   B Lack of communication creates serious problems.
   C Change occurs quickly and unexpectedly.
   D It is impossible to stop change.

9. Which suffix do you add to the word *doubt* to make a new word meaning "without a doubt"?

   A -able
   B -ment
   C -ful
   D -less

10. Read this passage from "Take NASA's World Wind for a Spin."

> NASA's World Wind brings the world to you in amazing detail. . . .
>
> Look at a bird's-eye view of streets and buildings in Washington, D.C.
>
> Use the collection of satellite images and information. More details and place names appear as you zoom in on an area.

Which sentence from the passage best explains the function of NASA's World Wind?

A *NASA's World Wind brings the world to you in amazing detail.*
B *Look at a bird's-eye view of streets and buildings in Washington, D.C.*
C *Use the collection of satellite images and information.*
D *More details and place names appear as you zoom in on an area.*

11. Which of the following best describes a theme of a story?

A an object that stands for an idea or feeling
B the main idea or message of a story
C the most exciting part of a story
D a word or group of words that are repeated in a story

12. Which of the following is the best example of a persuasive essay?

A an article about a famous environmentalist
B an article asking people to increase their recycling efforts
C an article describing a community cleanup event
D an article about the effects of global warming

13. Which suffix do you add to the word *pain* to make a new word that means "with a lot of pain"?

A -ful
B -less
C -able
D -ly

Read this passage from "Tracking the Bird Flu." Answer questions 14 and 15.

> I suggested that we visit the World Health Organization Web site and take a look at the maps. Sam could see from the maps that most of the cases of bird flu in people had occurred in Asia. The largest number of cases in chickens and other birds had occurred in Asia, too. I told Sam that the spread of the virus among birds did not assure that lots of people would get sick. It was not that easy to pass the virus from birds to humans.

14. Which sentence best describes a theme of this passage?

   A The World Health Organization has a Web site.

   B There are a lot of chickens in Asia.

   C The World Wide Web is a useful tool for doing research.

   D Bird flu is very common.

15. Which sentence from the passage is most important if you are reading to find out where cases of bird flu in humans most commonly occur?

   A *It was not that easy to pass the virus from birds to humans.*

   B *I told Sam that the spread of the virus among birds did not assure that lots of people would get sick.*

   C *The largest number of cases in chickens and other birds had occurred in Asia, too.*

   D *Sam could see from the maps that most of the cases of bird flu in people had occurred in Asia.*

Choose the word that best completes each sentence for questions 16 and 17.

16. The system of buying and selling products is known as _____.

   A commerce

   B machinery

   C network

   D cylinder

17. When you make something better than it was before, you _____ it.

   A cylinder

   B network

   C assure

   D improve

Read this passage from "Cast Your Vote for the Future." Answer questions 18 and 19.

> Third, the <u>Internet</u> is "the future," as it gets faster and easier to use. And more people get a chance to use it. Today, you can get telephone service over the Internet. You can download music and videos. Some radio stations send their broadcast over the Internet. You can watch television programs and movies online.

18. Which of the following details from the passage is most important if you are reading to find out how the Internet is changing?

    A Some radio and television stations broadcast on the Internet.
    B The Internet has music and videos.
    C The Internet gets faster and easier to use, and more people use it.
    D You can watch television online.

19. What does the word <u>Internet</u> mean in this passage?

    A a computer used by radio stations
    B a worldwide information system
    C a type of telephone service
    D a computer program used to make videos

Read this passage. The sentences are numbered. Answer questions 20 and 21.

> (1) Every Saturday morning, Jae-Min hurriedly runs over to the bowling alley down the street. (2) He spends half the day there, practicing his game. (3) He bowls _____ than anyone else our age. (4) He will probably be a professional bowler someday.

20. Which of the following words in sentence 1 is an adverb?

    A runs
    B morning
    C hurriedly
    D down

21. Which word best completes sentence 3?

    A better
    B best
    C great
    D greatest

Read this passage from "Take NASA's World Wind for a Spin." Answer questions 22 and 23.

> Control the globe's level of detail. Turn the lines of longitude and latitude and the country boundaries on or off. Tilt the globe in any angle. The names of places appear as you zoom in on the globe. . . .
>
> Track fires, floods, storms, dust, and smoke around the world. Navigate quickly using icons.

22. How can you figure out the name of a country using NASA's World Wind?

    A Turn the lines of longitude and latitude on or off.
    B Zoom in on the globe.
    C Use icons to locate areas that have experienced certain events.
    D Tilt the globe back and forth.

23. Which idea from the passage tells you about using World Wind to identify an area that has recently had a tornado?

    A You can adjust the globe's level of detail.
    B The names of places appear as you zoom in on the globe.
    C It helps you track storms.
    D You can tilt the globe in any angle.

Read this passage from "And Away We Go." Answer questions 24 and 25.

> Maria liked geography. She also loved her new computer. Her dad had said that doing research for her report would be a good way for Maria to check out the machine. Maria figured she shouldn't disagree. She had begged her parents for a laptop to replace her old computer, claiming it would be more <u>convenient</u>. . . .
>
> Maria typed "virtual globes" into the search engine. She sighed when she saw the dozens of Web pages on the list.

24. In this passage, the word <u>convenient</u> means —

    A easy to find   **C** difficult to find
    B easy to use   **D** difficult to use

25. What is the topic of Maria's report?

    A new computers   **C** virtual globes
    B geography   **D** her parents

Student _____   Date _____

Student Theme Progress Test Record

Skills Tested	Item Numbers (cross out numbers for items answered incorrectly)	Student Score	Criterion Score	If the student scored less than the Criterion Score, use these Reteaching Tools:
Comprehension Monitor Understanding: Reflect on Purpose	2 7 15 18 22 25	_____ of 6	5 / 6	**Monitor Understanding: Reflect on Purpose:** Comprehension Bridge 13
Determine Importance: Rank Information	10 23	_____ of 2	1 / 2	**Determine Importance: Rank Information:** Comprehension Bridge 12
Target Skill Identify Theme	8 11 14	_____ of 3	2 / 3	**Identify Theme:** Teacher's Guide p. 422
Vocabulary	16 17 19 24	_____ of 4	3 / 4	**Vocabulary:** During independent reading time, review student's Vocabulary Journal and discuss how to improve the journal entries
Word Study Suffixes *-ful, -able, -less*	4 9 13	_____ of 3	2 / 3	**Suffixes *-ful, -able, -less*:** Sourcebook p. 405 Teacher's Guide p. 420
Writing: Process Writing Process: Prewriting	6	_____ of 1	1 / 1	**Process: Prewriting:** Writing Bridge 25
Form: Persuasive Essay	3 12	_____ of 2	1 / 2	**Form: Persuasive Essay:** Writing Bridge 26
Writing: Grammar Adverbs: Regular and Special Comparison Forms	20 21	_____ of 2	1 / 2	**Adverbs: Regular and Special Comparison Forms:** Writing Resource Guide p. 25 Writer's Handbook p. 27
Prepositions	1 5	_____ of 2	1 / 2	**Prepositions:** Writing Resource Guide p. 28 Writer's Handbook p. 28
		_____ / 25	17 / 25	

Answer Key

1. C   2. B   3. A   4. B   5. D   6. C   7. B   8. A   9. D   10. A   11. B   12. B   13. A

14. C   15. D   16. A   17. D   18. C   19. B   20. C   21. A   22. B   23. C   24. B   25. C

THEME 14 Ongoing Test Practice

SAMPLE

Read the passage. Then answer the question.

A mirror is a piece of glass with a thin layer of aluminum on the back. When light hits the metal, it bounces off and creates a reflection. The glass on the mirror protects the metal from scratches.

S. Which sentence best summarizes this passage?

A You can see yourself in a mirror because light bounces off of a layer of aluminum.

B Mirrors are made mostly of metal, but there is a thin layer of glass behind the metal.

C The main part of a mirror is made of glass, which is there to protect the layer of metal.

D Mirrors are made of a layer of reflective aluminum and a protective sheet of glass.

Read the passage. Then read each question. Circle the letter of the correct answer.

The World Wide Web

A Web site is a group of pages that mix words and pictures you can see only on a computer. Some sites have only one page, while others have many pages. To view a Web page, you need a special computer program called a browser. Once you are connected to the Internet, you type the address of the Web site you want to visit into the browser, and it takes you there. The collection of all the Web sites in the world is known as the World Wide Web.

Where did the World Wide Web come from? About 50 years ago, the two most powerful countries in the world were the United States and the Soviet Union, and they were in the middle of the Cold War. The two countries were angry with each other but did not fight a war. However, the danger of war haunted everyone. The United States was worried that if there was a real war, the military might not be able to get information from computers that were far away. Some scientists got together and figured out a way to let computers talk to one another. The new system was called ARPANET.

In 1972 a man named Ray Tomlinson created the first e-mail program. His invention allowed people to send messages back and forth electronically. As the worldwide network got better, more people started using computers. ARPANET became known as the Internet.

In the 1980s people starting getting computers for their homes. Soon people were sending e-mail back and forth regularly. Then in 1989, the World Wide Web was created. Like the discovery of fire, the Web changed people's lives.

The Web is an information superhighway. It allows people to share their thoughts with the whole world. Now companies advertise on the Internet, and millions of people all over the world use the World Wide Web to find news stories, research information, buy and sell things, and more. It is an incredibly useful tool.

1. Which of the following best summarizes the first paragraph of the passage?

   A   A Web site consists of pictures and words.
   B   A Web site is a collection of pages you can see only by using a browser and the Internet.
   C   To view a Web site, you need to use a computer that is connected to the Internet.
   D   You can go to any Web site you want if you know its address.

2. Which sentence from the passage contains an analogy?

   A   *Soon people were sending e-mail back and forth regularly.*
   B   *The collection of all the Web sites in the world is known as the World Wide Web.*
   C   *Like the discovery of fire, the Web changed people's lives.*
   D   *The Web is an information superhighway.*

3. What does the word <u>invention</u> mean in this passage?

   A   something new a person makes
   B   something made for a computer
   C   something a person improves
   D   something sold on the Web

4. Which of the following best describes why the World Wide Web became popular?

   A   Companies advertise on it.
   B   It was created in 1989.
   C   Almost anybody can use it.
   D   You need a browser to use it.

5. Which of the following sentences from the passage contains a metaphor?

   A   *Then in 1989, the World Wide Web was created.*
   B   *It allows people to share their thoughts with the whole world.*
   C   *The new system was called ARPANET.*
   D   *The Web is an information superhighway.*

Answer the following question on a separate sheet of paper.

6. Using information from the passage, explain why scientists created ARPANET.

THEME 14 Theme Progress Test

Read each question. Fill in the correct circle on your answer document.

1. When you summarize a passage, you —

   A decide which idea is most important and which idea is least important
   B bring a text's big ideas together into a short, meaningful description
   C try to figure out the author's reason for writing the passage
   D explain how the plot is similar to or different from the plot of another passage

2. Which of the following words means "in a pleasant way"?

   A pleasantly
   B pleasantness
   C unpleasantly
   D unpleasant

3. Read this passage from "Bill Gates."

   > In 1968, computers were huge and complicated. They were also very expensive. Thus, most schools could not afford to own a computer. Lakeside School raised a few thousand dollars to buy time on a computer owned by General Electric. General Electric charged the school based on the number of hours students used the computer.

   Which sentence best summarizes this passage?

   A Computers were huge, complicated machines in 1968.
   B Lakeside School was the first school to purchase a computer for its students.
   C General Electric owned a huge, complicated, and expensive computer that the students used in 1968.
   D In 1968 Lakeside School raised thousands of dollars so students could use a computer owned by General Electric.

4. What is the root of the word *celebration*?

   A celebrity   **C** celebrating
   B celebrate   **D** ration

5. Which sentence is written correctly?

    A My mother asked Dr. Peterson "if I was sick?"

    B My mother asked dr. peterson if I was sick.

    C My mother asked Dr. Peterson if I was sick.

    D My mother asked Dr. Peterson if I was sick!

6. Read this passage from "Emilia and the Birthday Party."

> Emilia sat down at the dinner table, a huge smile on her face. The day had been like a fairy tale. Still, she had learned a lesson. Emilia decided that she'd never put off doing her chores until the last minute again.

Which sentence best summarizes this passage?

    A Emilia was happy that everything turned out all right, but she promised herself that she would never ignore her chores that long again.

    B Emilia had a great day and learned a lesson.

    C Emilia felt that the day had been a lot like a fairy tale when she got home and sat down at the dinner table.

    D Emilia decided not to put off doing her chores, and she learned a lesson.

7. Which suffix do you add to the word *entertain* to make a new word meaning "the act of keeping people entertained"?

    A -ness   **C** -tion

    B -ion   **D** -ment

8. Read this passage from "Emilia and the Birthday Party."

> "Eight," Emilia grumbled. "And I still have one stack of dishes, and the windows and floors, and my room. . . ."
>
> The fairy godmother broke in, growing impatient, "All right! So, we need a washing machine that can do eight loads of laundry at once, a huge dishwasher, and a Winfloor-Clutter-Buster."

Why is it important to understand what a Winfloor-Clutter-Buster is?

    A It helps you figure out how the fairy godmother helps Emilia.

    B It helps you determine who the fairy godmother is.

    C It helps you figure out why Emilia needs the fairy godmother's help.

    D It helps you determine where the fairy godmother came from.

9. Read this passage from "Hank, Make Your Bed!"

> That did it. I decided to invent a bed-making machine that would solve my problem and those of kids throughout the world with tidy mothers who find enjoyment in neatness. I'd be rich enough to retire before I even hit labor-force age!

Which sentence best summarizes this passage?

A The speaker thinks that a lot of kids will be interested in a bed-making machine.

B The speaker imagines that he will invent something very useful.

C The speaker worries about kids throughout the world who have tidy mothers.

D The speaker believes he can get rich and help kids by inventing a bed-making machine.

10. Which suffix should you add to the word *delight* to make a new word that means "in a way that is full of delight"?

A -ly   **C** -ion

B -fully   **D** -tion

11. If you wanted to write an essay about the things you and your friends have in common, which method of organizing ideas should you use?

A sequence of events

B compare and contrast

C cause and effect

D problem to solution

12. Read this passage from "Emilia and the Birthday Party."

> Emilia wanted to start getting ready to go right after breakfast. But all of a sudden she groaned and sat down on her bed with a thump. Emilia had put off doing her chores all week. Now she had mountains of laundry and dishes to do, floors to scrub, windows to wash, and her whole room to clean.

Which sentence best summarizes this passage?

A Emilia realizes she must finish her chores before she can go to the party.

B Emilia has put off her chores all week, and now she must complete them.

C Emilia is excited and wants to get ready, but instead she sits on her bed and groans.

D Emilia was supposed to do her chores, but she put them off for later.

13. What suffix can you add to the word *logical* to make a new word that means "in a logical manner"?

A -ly   C -ness

B -ion   D -ment

Read this passage from "Bill Gates." Answer questions 14 and 15.

In 1975, when Bill was 19, he and Paul Allen formed Microsoft. The team launched their software company at the right time. Personal computers were just coming on the market. They all needed software to run.

Bill Gates believes success requires hard work. He says that if you are smart and know how to apply what you know, you can accomplish anything. This belief was certainly true for Bill Gates. Microsoft's success has grown along with computer sales.

14. Why did Microsoft become a successful company?

A It was the only company that sold computers.

B It was started by two young men in 1975.

C It offered a product that a lot of people needed.

D It showed people that anyone could do well in business.

15. Which detail from the passage is most important if you are reading to find out what Bill Gates believes makes a person successful?

A Bill Gates was 19 years old when he and Paul Allen formed Microsoft.

B Bill Gates says you can accomplish anything if you are smart and apply what you know.

C Bill Gates and Paul Allen launched Microsoft at the right time.

D Microsoft's success has grown as computer sales have increased.

Choose the word that best completes each sentence for questions 16 and 17.

16. To amaze or greatly surprise people is to _____ them.

A risk   C astonish

B simplify   D manufacture

17. If you want to be the only person who can sell something that you created, you need to get _____.

A a patent   C an invention

B a device   D a brand

Read this passage. The sentences are numbered. Answer questions 18 and 19.

> (1) Rena will not be in school today. (2) She has a sore throat, and her doctor says she'll have to wait until Thursday to return to school.

18. Which contraction best combines two words from sentence 1?

   A wasn't

   B willn't

   C wouldn't

   D won't

19. Which pair of words in sentence 2 forms a prepositional phrase?

   A until Thursday

   B her doctor

   C to wait

   D sore throat

Read this excerpt from "Hank, Make Your Bed!" Answer questions 20 and 21.

> "Hank, did you . . . ?" Mom called upstairs from the kitchen, which doubles as her control center for tracking family members.
> "Don't I every single day?" I responded with a hint of resentment.
> "Is it as neat as possible?" she asked.
> "Just as a cumulus cloud is lovely and puffy, so is my bed," I replied, trying to make her laugh.
> Mom knit her eyebrows. "Hmmm. Puffy isn't exactly neat."

20. Which line from the passage includes a metaphor?

   A *"Hank, did you . . . ?"*

   B *Mom called upstairs from the kitchen, which doubles as her control center for tracking family members.*

   C *"Is it as neat as possible?"*

   D *Mom knit her eyebrows.*

21. Which line from the passage contains an analogy?

   A *"Don't I every single day?"*

   B *I responded with a hint of resentment.*

   C *"Just as a cumulus cloud is lovely and puffy, so is my bed," I replied, trying to make her laugh.*

   D *"Hmmm. Puffy isn't exactly neat."*

Read this passage from "Bill Gates." Answer questions 22 and 23.

How many computers does your school have? Do you have one at home? Does your public library have computers? Not so long ago personal computers were only a dream. Now they seem to be everywhere. But computers might not be so popular if it weren't for people like Bill Gates. Gates, like many others, helped improve and <u>simplify</u> computer technology.

22. Which sentence from this passage contains a metaphor?

  A *How many computers does your school have?*

  B *Not so long ago personal computers were only a dream.*

  C *Now they seem to be everywhere.*

  D *But computers might not be so popular if it weren't for people like Bill Gates.*

23. What does the word <u>simplify</u> mean in this passage?

  A make popular

  B make cheaper

  C make harder

  D make easier

Read this passage from "Lives Spun of Silk." Answer questions 24 and 25.

"I spin," said Spider.
"I invent," said Human Being.
"Our work has filled our lives with <u>ease</u>."
"My threads help me move and swing here and there."
"I travel in trains, planes, and automobiles."

24. In what way are the spider and the human being alike?

  A They both spin silk threads.

  B They both travel in automobiles.

  C They both do things that make their lives easier.

  D They both invent things.

25. What is the meaning of the word <u>ease</u>?

  A with some difficulty

  B with no difficulty

  C with some work

  D with no work

THEME 14

Student Theme Progress Test Record

Skills Tested	Item Numbers (cross out numbers for items answered incorrectly)	Student Score	Criterion Score	If the student scored less than the Criterion Score, use these Reteaching Tools:
Comprehension Synthesize: Create a Summary	1 3 6 9 12 14	___ of 6	5 / 6	**Synthesize: Create a Summary:** Comprehension Bridge 14
Monitor Understanding: Reflect on Purpose	8 15	___ of 2	1 / 2	**Monitor Understanding: Reflect on Purpose:** Comprehension Bridge 13
Target Skill Identify Analogies	21	___ of 1	1 / 1	**Identify Analogies:** Teacher's Guide p. 445
Understand Metaphor	20 22	___ of 2	1 / 2	**Understand Metaphor:** Teacher's Guide p. 454
Vocabulary	16 17 23 25	___ of 4	3 / 4	**Vocabulary:** During independent reading time, review student's Vocabulary Journal and discuss how to improve the journal entries
Word Study Suffixes *-ness, -ion, -tion,* and *-ment*	4 7 13	___ of 3	2 / 3	**Suffixes *-ness, -ion, -tion,* and *-ment*** Sourcebook p. 423 Teacher's Guide p. 436
Suffixes *-ly, -fully*	2 10	___ of 2	1 / 2	**Suffixes *-ly, -fully*:** Sourcebook p. 435 Teacher's Guide p. 452
Writing: Process Writing Trait: Conventions	5	___ of 1	1 / 1	**Trait: Conventions:** Writing Bridge 27
Organizational Pattern: Compare and Contrast	11 24	___ of 2	1 / 2	**Organizational Pattern: Compare and Contrast:** Writing Bridge 28
Writing: Grammar Contractions	18	___ of 1	1 / 1	**Contractions:** Writing Resource Guide p. 27 Writer's Handbook p. 18
Prepositions and Prepositional Phrases	19	___ of 1	1 / 1	**Prepositions and Prepositional Phrases:** Writing Resource Guide p. 28 Writer's Handbook p. 28
		___ / 25	18 / 25	

Answer Key

1. B   2. A   3. D   4. B   5. C   6. A   7. D   8. A   9. D   10. B   11. B   12. A   13. A

14. C   15. B   16. C   17. A   18. D   19. A   20. D   21. C   22. B   23. D   24. C   25. B

THEME 15 Ongoing Test Practice

SAMPLE
Read the passage. Then answer the question.

Mount Rushmore is a memorial to four of our country's greatest presidents. If you go to the Black Hills in South Dakota, you can see giant carvings of the faces of George Washington, Thomas Jefferson, Abraham Lincoln, and Theodore Roosevelt.

S. Looking at a picture of people standing in front of Mount Rushmore would help you imagine —

    A where the Black Hills are located in South Dakota
    B how big the faces on Mount Rushmore are
    C the name of the person who carved Mount Rushmore
    D when the faces were carved into Mount Rushmore

Read the passage. Then read each question. Circle the letter of the correct answer.

The Best Inventions

"Today we're going to discuss inventions," Mrs. Kwan announced. "Can anybody give me some examples of inventions that have made our lives easier?"

The silence in the room told her that nobody wanted to talk first. Finally, Andy raised his hand and said, "How about the microwave oven? It helps us defrost and cook food quickly."

"What about the Internet?" Juanita suggested. "It lets us find all kinds of information quickly. You can also use the Internet to communicate with people far away."

"My family has a Web page," Kim added. "It has pictures of all of us, and we each write stuff for it. We can even <u>arrange</u> to meet my grandma online to chat about what is happening in our lives."

"I think the best invention is the lightbulb," Dylan said. "It's something we all use every day. Lightbulbs are in lamps, streetlights, automobiles, and even refrigerators!"

"Good example!" Mrs. Kwan responded. "The lightbulb was invented by Thomas Edison, one of the most famous inventors in history. He also invented the phonograph, which was the first machine that could record sounds, the motion picture camera for making movies, and an early type of alkaline battery."

Jenelle asked, "Where did he learn how to invent all that cool stuff?"

"He just thought about problems people had and worked hard to figure out ways to fix them," Mrs. Kwan answered. "A lot of the time, the machines he made didn't work, or people didn't want to buy them. But when he came up with a really good idea, not only did it work—it changed the world."

1. Thinking about the picture of Thomas Edison helps you understand that he —

   A believed nobody would like the lightbulb

   B wished he had invented the telephone

   C thought his phonograph was a great invention

   D was proud of his electric lightbulb

2. What does the word <u>arrange</u> mean in this passage?

   A to do something as a family

   B to talk with someone far away

   C to make plans to do something

   D to show someone a picture

3. The diagram of the lightbulb in the picture helps you imagine —

   A where the lightbulb was invented

   B how a lightbulb works

   C where you can buy lightbulbs

   D how hot a lightbulb gets

4. Which sentence from the passage includes an example of personification?

   A *The silence in the room told her that nobody wanted to talk first.*

   B *"It has pictures of all of us, and we each write stuff for it."*

   C *"Where did he learn how to invent all that cool stuff?"*

   D *"You can also use the Internet to communicate with people far away."*

5. Which sentence from the passage includes an interjection?

   A *"It lets us find all kinds of information quickly."*

   B *"My family has a Web page," Kim added.*

   C *"How about the microwave oven?"*

   D *"Good example!" Mrs. Kwan responded.*

Answer the following question on a separate sheet of paper.

6. Use the illustration and information from the passage to explain how people probably felt when they first saw an electric light.

THEME ⑮ Theme Progress Test

Read each question. Fill in the correct circle on your answer document.

1. Which of the following is an example of a closed compound word?

   A well-respected   **C** overboard

   B real estate   **D** computer

2. What does the word <u>emerge</u> mean in the passage below?

   > Every year on February 2, people gather in Punxsutawney, Pennsylvania, to see the groundhog <u>emerge</u> from his hole in the ground. They say that if he sees his shadow, there will be six more weeks of winter.

   A to gather in a crowd

   B to live underground

   C to go into something

   D to come out of something

3. Read these lines from the poem "Five Spring Flowers."

   > Five spring flowers, [standing] all in a row.
   > The first one said, "We need rain to grow!"

   This poem includes an example of —

   A metaphor   **C** simile

   B slang   **D** personification

4. What does it mean to use visuals to create images as you read?

   A use visuals to help you create a picture in your mind and understand a text

   B use visuals to help you predict what will happen next in a text

   C use visuals to help you connect a text to other texts, yourself, and the world

   D use visuals to help you better understand the author's purpose for writing

5. Which list of words contains all conjunctions?

   A shake, respond, spy

   B although, either, nor

   C banana, foot, puppet

   D quickly, well, less

6. If you combine the words *fire* and *place*, what does the new word mean?

   A someplace where you can have a fire
   B a place that is on fire
   C a fire that is burning someplace
   D someplace that was once on fire

7. When you are ready to share your writing with others, you should —

   A get rid of the margins on the pages
   B create a graphic organizer
   C make sure it is neatly written
   D write a list of your ideas

8. Read this passage from "Amazing Bamboo."

> I have chosen bamboo as the subject of my observation log. Bamboo is an amazing plant. Although it looks like a shrub or a tree, bamboo is actually a member of the grass family. There are more than 1,000 different types of bamboo. Some types grow to less than a foot tall. Other types can grow to over 100 feet tall.

What does the illustration accompanying this passage help you imagine?

   A some different ways that people use bamboo
   B what a bamboo forest might look like
   C the different parts of the world where bamboo grows
   D why bamboo grows so much taller than grass

9. You would most likely write a formal letter to —

   A your cousin
   B a good friend
   C your grandmother
   D a business

10. Which of the following sentences includes personification?

   A Raindrops danced down my umbrella during the storm.
   B The red rooster ran rapidly from the barnyard.
   C The balloon exploded with a loud pop.
   D The room in the basement looked as dark as night.

11. Read this passage from "Inside Job."

> He studied charts and turned on sensors. Then he pushed a button, and giant cutters came out of the submarine. Ali also saw what looked like giant pliers emerge. For the next hour, the submarine moved from one part of the DNA to another, cutting pieces in one place and attaching them in another.

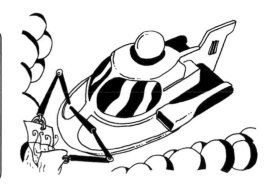

What does the illustration with this passage help you imagine?

A where the submarine goes

B why Ali and her dad are changing the DNA

C how the arms of the submarine work

D who invented the submarine

12. Which of the following is an example of an open compound word?

A user-friendly

B running shoes

C blackboard

D medicine

13. Read this passage from "Amazing Bamboo."

> Bamboo does not grow like a tree. An individual tree gets taller and its trunk gets bigger around each year. An individual bamboo stem—or cane—grows to its full height and weight in about five or eight weeks. This is true even for the tallest canes.

Which of the following sentences best summarizes this passage?

A Bamboo is a plant, like a tree, but it doesn't grow like a tree.

B Unlike a tree, which gets taller and wider each year, bamboo grows to its full height in a matter of weeks.

C The tall part of the bamboo plant is called a stem, or a cane.

D Every year, a tree gets taller and wider around the trunk, but bamboo grows in a very different way.

Read these lines from the poem "Five Spring Flowers." Answer questions 14 and 15.

> Then BOOM! went the thunder
> And ZAP! went the lightning!
> That springtime storm was really frightening!
> But the flowers weren't worried—no, no, no, NO!
> The rain helped them to grow, grow, GROW!

14. Which line from the poem includes the best example of personification?

   A *Then BOOM! went the thunder*

   B *That springtime storm was really frightening!*

   C *But the flowers weren't worried—no, no, no, NO!*

   D *The rain helped them to grow, grow, GROW!*

15. In this poem, *no, no, no, No!* is an example of —

   A compound words   **C** conjunctions

   B interjections   **D** a metaphor

Read this passage from the story "Inside Job." Answer questions 16 and 17.

> Ali couldn't contain her excitement. Several years before, her father had developed a method of shrinking a submarine smaller than a <u>cell</u>. Using the sub, he could enter a fruit cell and change its DNA. His company now produced the world's tastiest fruit! Today her father was going to change DNA to produce a larger, sweeter orange, and Ali was going along!

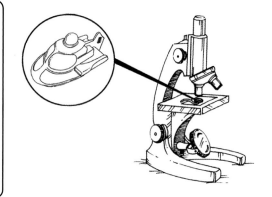

16. The illustration in this passage helps you imagine —

   A the size of the submarine Ali's father created

   B where Ali's father plans to drive the submarine

   C the place where Ali's father's company is located

   D how the submarine will change the orange's DNA

17. What does the word <u>cell</u> mean in this passage?

   A a place where fruit is stored

   B a place where a submarine is stored

   C the largest, most complex part of something

   D the smallest, simplest part of something

Read this passage from "Amazing Bamboo." Answer questions 18 and 19.

April 20, 4:45 P.M.
Bamboo Shoot 1: 229 inches (19 feet 1 inch) tall
Bamboo Shoot 2: 268 inches (22 feet 4 inches) tall
Observation: Shoot 2 has topped 22 feet in less than 20 days. Both shoots have about 40 more days to grow during the season. At this rate, Shoot 2 should reach 50 feet tall by the end of the growing season.

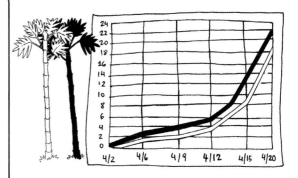

18. The graph in this passage helps you imagine —

   A how fast each bamboo shoot grew
   B why one bamboo shoot grew faster
   C what a 50-foot tall bamboo shoot looks like
   D what bamboo shoots feel like

19. Which sentence best summarizes this passage?

   A There are two bamboo shoots being measured, and one is growing faster than the other one.
   B Bamboo Shoot 2 has grown taller than Bamboo Shoot 1 and will likely grow to be about 50 feet tall.
   C About 40 days after April 20, Bamboo Shoot 2 will be done growing and will be about 50 feet tall.
   D Bamboo Shoot 1 is a little more than 19 feet tall, and it will continue to grow over the next 40 days.

Choose the word that best completes each sentence for questions 20 and 21.

20. The study of all living things is known as _____.

   A nucleus   **C** biology
   B specimen   **D** division

21. If you wanted to keep something in a safe place until later, you would put it in _____.

   A storage   **C** detail
   B division   **D** element

Read this passage from "We Would Like to Invite You . . ." Answer questions 22 and 23.

> Dear Dr. Silva:
> . . . I have enclosed a map to Rigby [Elementary School] in hopes that you will be able to fit us into your schedule. Either call me at 555-2783 or respond via e-mail, please. I look forward to hearing from you.
> Sincerely,
> Sue Miller

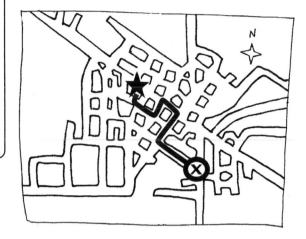

★ Rigby Elementary School
X Dr. Silva

22. This passage is an example of —

   A   an informal letter
   B   a newspaper article
   C   a formal letter
   D   an observation log

23. The map in this passage can be used to help you imagine —

   A   the population of the town
   B   the number of students who attend Rigby Elementary School
   C   the number of miles Dr. Silva must drive
   D   the path Dr. Silva will take to get to Rigby Elementary School

Read this passage. The sentences are numbered. Answer questions 24 and 25.

> (1) Hanging a horseshoe over a doorway is considered by many people to bring luck, _____ you have to be careful how you hang it. (2) If you hang it with the ends pointing up, it is good luck. (3) If you hang it with the ends pointing down, it is bad luck.

24. Which word best completes sentence 1?

   A   either   C   or
   B   but   D   nor

25. Which of these groups of words from the passage can be an independent clause?

   A   *Hanging a horseshoe over a doorway*
   B   *If you hang it*
   C   *with the ends pointing up*
   D   *it is bad luck*

THEME 15

Student Theme Progress Test Record

Skills Tested	Item Numbers (cross out numbers for items answered incorrectly)	Student Score	Criterion Score	If the student scored less than the Criterion Score, use these Reteaching Tools:
Comprehension Create Images: Use Visuals	4 8 11 16 18 23	_____ of 6	5 / 6	**Create Images: Use Visuals:** Comprehension Bridge 15
Synthesize: Create a Summary	13 19	_____ of 2	1 / 2	**Synthesize: Create a Summary:** Comprehension Bridge 14
Target Skill Understand Personification	3 10 14	_____ of 3	2 / 3	**Understand Personification:** Teacher's Guide p. 488
Vocabulary	2 17 20 21	_____ of 4	3 / 4	**Vocabulary:** During independent reading time, review student's Vocabulary Journal and discuss how to improve the journal entries
Word Study Compound Words	1 6 12	_____ of 3	2 / 3	**Compound Words:** Sourcebook p. 467 Teacher's Guide p. 486
Writing: Process Writing Trait: Presentation	7	_____ of 1	1 / 1	**Trait: Presentation:** Writing Bridge 29
Form: Letter	9 22	_____ of 2	1 / 2	**Form: Letter:** Writing Bridge 30
Writing: Grammar Conjunctions: Coordinate and Subordinate	24	_____ of 1	1 / 1	**Conjunctions: Coordinate and Subordinate:** Writing Resource Guide p. 29 Writer's Handbook p. 29
Conjunctions and Interjections	5 15	_____ of 2	1 / 2	**Conjunctions and Interjections:** Writing Resource Guide p. 29 Writer's Handbook p. 29
Independent and Dependent Clauses	25	_____ of 1	1 / 1	**Independent and Dependent Clauses:** Writing Resource Guide p. 30 Writer's Handbook p. 36
		_____ / 25	18 / 25	

Answer Key

1. C   2. D   3. D   4. A   5. B   6. A   7. C   8. B   9. D   10. A   11. C   12. B   13. B

14. C   15. B   16. A   17. D   18. A   19. B   20. C   21. A   22. C   23. D   24. B   25. D

THEME 16 **Ongoing Test Practice**

SAMPLE
Read the passage. Then answer the question.

Although sunlight appears to be clear, it actually contains red, orange, yellow, green, blue, and violet light. When there is a lot of water in the air, such as after a storm, the drops of water refract the sunlight. The sunlight gets separated into bands of color and forms a rainbow.

S. What happens to light when it is refracted?

A It is reflected back into space.
B It is broken up into different parts by raindrops.
C It is absorbed by drops of water.
D It turns into drops of rain as it falls.

Read the passage. Then read each question. Circle the letter of the correct answer.

Gregor Mendel, the Father of Genetics

Johann Mendel was born on July 20, 1822, in what is now the Czech Republic. As a child and young adult, he enjoyed spending time in the garden, taking care of plants and flowers. When he grew up, he became a monk and lived in a monastery. He continued his religious studies and became a priest a few years later. After being ordained, Johann Mendel changed his name to Gregor Mendel.

Like many other priests, Mendel wanted to be a teacher. He went to several universities to study with professors. Unfortunately, he had a lot of trouble passing the certification test. This meant he could not become a teacher. However, in his studies, he learned a lot about science and research. He remembered how much he enjoyed working as a gardener. This inspired him to study plants.

For about seven years, Mendel experimented with nearly 30,000 pea plants. He took notes about the traits of different types of pea plants. He then mixed the plants together in many different ways to see how they would grow. He learned that some characteristics of a plant, such as its color or size, appeared no matter how he mixed the plant with other plants. Mendel also noted that other characteristics showed up only some of the time. Additionally, he realized that no matter how many ways he combined pea plants, the new plants that grew showed only the traits of the original plants. For example, if he took two plants that always grew short, he could never get them to grow tall. To make a plant grow tall, he had to start with at least one plant that already grew tall.

Mendel published a paper about his discoveries, but people were not very interested in it, and it was largely forgotten. A few years later, he became an abbot. As the head monk, he spent most of his time running the monastery and rarely worked with plants. He died on January 6, 1884.

A few decades later, scientists rediscovered Mendel's work. This time they were very interested in what he had done. His discoveries were the <u>basic</u> building blocks that led to the creation of the science of genetics. Thanks to the work of Gregor Mendel, people today have a better understanding of how traits are passed from parents to children.

1. Based on information in the passage, you can tell that a *monk* is —

   A someone who changes his or her name
   B a person who enjoys working in a garden
   C a religious person who lives in a monastery
   D someone who was born in the Czech Republic

2. What does the word <u>basic</u> mean in this passage?

   A most important
   B in the middle
   C least important
   D very last

3. You can tell from the passage that in order to become a teacher, Mendel had to —

   A study how plants grow
   B spend time in a monastery
   C learn how to do scientific research
   D pass a certification test

4. Which sentence in paragraph 1 foreshadows Mendel's scientific work?

   A *Johann Mendel was born on July 20, 1822, in what is now the Czech Republic.*
   B *As a child and young adult, he enjoyed spending time in the garden, taking care of plants and flowers.*
   C *He continued his religious studies and became a priest a few years later.*
   D *After being ordained, Johann Mendel changed his name to Gregor Mendel.*

5. Based on paragraph 4 of the passage, you can tell that an *abbot* is —

   A a person who studies genetics
   B a person who is in charge of a monastery
   C a person who studies plants
   D a person who makes an important discovery

Answer the following question on a separate sheet of paper.

6. Why did Mendel give up his scientific research?

THEME 16 **Theme Progress Test**

Read each question. Fill in the correct circle on your answer document.

1. What does it mean to read on in a text?

   A to identify the author of the text
   B to put ideas in the text together and form a new idea
   C to read to find the author's purpose for writing
   D to read past a difficult word or idea to help you figure out the meaning

2. Read these lines from the poem "The Circulatory Ride."

   > I feel the pressure begin to mount,
   > One by one my steps I count.
   > The other blood cells laugh and shout,
   > Happily eager for the wild ride no doubt.
   > A gentle float is more my speed.

   The illustration with this poem helps show —

   A what the blood's path looks like
   B the health of the heart in the picture
   C why blood is important for life
   D how long it takes blood to travel through the body

3. Which word best completes the chart below?

break	joke	hop
breaking	joking	?

   A hoping
   B hopeing
   C hopping
   D hoped

4. What is the past tense form of the verb *think*?

   A thank
   B thought
   C thinked
   D thanked

5. Read this passage from "Something to Sneeze About!"

> Tony opened his notebook and wrote the date at the top of the page.
> Mrs. Figueroa said, "Start now. I'll tell you when time is up." Then she opened
> the large terrarium that sat in front of the windows and began checking
> on her many plants.

By reading on, you can figure out that a terrarium is —

A a type of window

B something used to measure time

C a place where notebooks are kept

D something that holds plants

6. For which word below should you double the final consonant when adding the suffix -*er*?

A row

B cook

C run

D lift

7. When you write a story, you should include —

A true facts about a recent event

B characters based on people who really exist

C characters and a setting

D lines that include rhythm and rhyme

8. What is the past tense form of the verb *grow*?

A growed

B grew

C grewed

D growing

9. What does it mean to edit your writing?

A to neatly write your final draft

B to make a graphic organizer

C to include details that support your main idea

D to check your spelling and punctuation

10. Read this passage from "Smart Food, Smart Choices, Healthy You!"

> Unsaturated fat is sometimes called "heart healthy" fat. It's found in olive oil, peanut oil, canola oil, and fish such as salmon and tuna. Eating foods with unsaturated fat is a smart choice. Saturated fats are found in meat, poultry, and dairy products. Eating too much saturated fat is not good for you.

By reading on, you can determine that unsaturated fat is —

A a healthy kind of fat

B an unhealthy kind of fat

C a kind of fat found in meat

D a kind of fat found in dairy products

11. What is the past tense form of the verb *shake*?

A shakes

B shook

C shaked

D shaken

12. Which of the following sentences is written correctly?

A My neighbor Mr. Adams has lived on Oak Road for 12 years.

B My neighbor, Mr. Adams has lived on Oak Road, four 12 years.

C My neighbor mr. adams has lived on oak road for 12 years.

D My neighbor mr. Adams has lived on Oak Road for 12 years

13. Which of the following best describes the plot of a story?

A a list of the main and secondary characters in a story

B a problem and a series of events that solves the problem

C a description of where and when a story takes place

D an explanation of why an author decided to write a story

14. What does the word <u>defend</u> mean in the sentence below?

> When a stranger knocked on the door, the dog jumped up and started growling, ready to <u>defend</u> its family.

A to greet

B to escape

C to protect

D to hide

15. Read this passage from "Something to Sneeze About!"

> Rodney got up to sharpen his pencil at the sharpener on the windowsill. The grinding of the sharpener was followed by the sound of coughing. Rodney coughed and covered his mouth in the way they'd been taught in school to keep from spreading any germs. By the time he got back to his seat, his coughing had stopped.
>
> That reminded Tony of something. He remembered writing about someone coughing the other day. He flipped back in his science notebook. Sure enough, someone over by the window had coughed. Then today, Rodney coughed when he was in pretty much the same place.

Which of the following sentences from the passage is an example of flashback?

A *By the time he got back to his seat, his coughing had stopped.*

B *Then today, Rodney coughed when he was in pretty much the same place.*

C *The grinding of the sharpener was followed by the sound of coughing.*

D *He remembered writing about someone coughing the other day.*

Read these lines from the poem "The Circulatory Ride." Answer questions 16 and 17.

> Miles of arteries, capillaries, and veins
> Are the <u>circulatory</u> system's blood-filled lanes.
> Outward bound arteries pound and gush,
> But I much prefer the veins' lack of rush.
> The gentle return home is more my speed.

16. By reading on, you can determine that arteries are —

A small cells that cause the heart to beat

B small cells found in blood

C tubes that carry blood away from the heart

D tubes that carry blood back to the heart

17. What does the word <u>circulatory</u> mean in this poem?

A having to do with the movement of blood

B having to do with moving quickly

C having to do with traveling outward

D having to do with traveling a long distance

Read this passage from "Smart Food, Smart Choices, Healthy You!"
Answer questions 18 and 19.

> Your body also needs vitamins. However, your body can't make vitamins. It gets vitamins from the food you eat. Vitamin A gives you healthy skin and eyes and helps you resist infections. Smart choices for vitamin A include eggs, milk, sweet potatoes, and spinach. The different B vitamins are important for energy.

18. By reading on, you can figure out that vitamin A —

    A helps your body make vitamin B

    B helps your body produce oxygen

    C helps you see better

    D helps give you energy

19. The illustration of the food pyramid helps you understand —

    A how much you should eat of certain foods

    B why it is important to eat food

    C some different places to get food

    D the times of day you should eat certain foods

Choose the word that best completes each sentence for questions 20 and 21.

20. A mass of tissue that is responsible for moving a body part is called a _____.

    A lung

    B muscle

    C situation

    D substance

21. A particular area of interest, skill, or knowledge is a person's _____.

    A situation

    B respiratory

    C substance

    D specialization

Read this passage from "The Tale of Achilles: A Greek Myth." Answer questions 22 and 23.

> Once, in the lands of ancient Greece, there was a mortal man named Peleus (PEEL-e-us). He married Thetis (THEE-tus), a beautiful nymph, or sea-spirit. They had a son, Achilles (ah-KILL-ees). While he was still an infant, Thetis decided to try to make her son immortal. She did this by dipping the baby in the River Styx, the river of the Underworld. Wherever the wondrous waters touched Achilles, no weapon would be able to harm him. However, as she dipped him in the river, she held him by one heel. That heel did not get wet. As a result, he had one heel that remained mortal and vulnerable.

22. At the end of this story, Achilles is hit in the heel by an arrow and dies. Which sentence from this passage foreshadows this event?

   A *She did this by dipping the baby in the River Styx, the river of the Underworld.*
   B *As a result, he had one heel that remained mortal and vulnerable.*
   C *He married Thetis, a beautiful nymph, or sea-spirit.*
   D *Once, in the lands of ancient Greece, there was a mortal man named Peleus.*

23. By reading on, you can determine that a person who is immortal —

   A is an infant
   B is a sea-spirit
   C cannot die from an injury
   D cannot swim

Read this passage. The sentences are numbered. Answer questions 24 and 25.

> (1) Denny and Tim work for a mining company. (2) They are the hardest working _____ in the whole mine. (3) Everyone appreciates _____ hard work.

24. Which word best completes sentence 2?

   A pair   C pare
   B payer   D pear

25. Which word best completes sentence 3?

   A there   C these
   B they're   D their

Student _____ Date _____

THEME 16

Student Theme Progress Test Record

Skills Tested	Item Numbers (cross out numbers for items answered incorrectly)	Student Score	Criterion Score	If the student scored less than the Criterion Score, use these Reteaching Tools:
Comprehension Use Fix-Up Strategies: Read On	1 5 10 16 18 23	____ of 6	5 / 6	**Use Fix-Up Strategies: Read On:** Comprehension Bridge 16
Create Images: Use Visuals	2 19	____ of 2	1 / 2	**Create Images: Use Visuals:** Comprehension Bridge 15
Target Skill Identify Plot	13	____ of 1	1 / 1	**Identify Plot:** Teacher's Guide p. 511
Identify Foreshadowing and Flashback	15 22	____ of 2	1 / 2	**Identify Foreshadowing and Flashback:** Teacher's Guide p. 520
Vocabulary	14 17 20 21	____ of 4	3 / 4	**Vocabulary:** During independent reading time, review student's Vocabulary Journal and discuss how to improve the journal entries
Word Study Consonant Doubling	3 6	____ of 2	1 / 2	**Consonant Doubling:** Sourcebook p. 485 Teacher's Guide p. 502
Writing: Process Writing Process: Editing	9 12	____ of 2	1 / 2	**Process: Editing:** Writing Bridge 31
Form: Story	7	____ of 1	1 / 1	**Form: Story:** Writing Bridge 32
Writing: Grammar Homophones	24	____ of 1	1 / 1	**Homophones:** Writing Resource Guide p. 31 Writer's Handbook p. 31
Commonly Misused Words	25	____ of 1	1 / 1	**Commonly Misused Words:** Writing Resource Guide p. 32 Writer's Handbook p. 50
Irregular Verbs	4 8 11	____ of 3	2 / 3	**Irregular Verbs:** Writing Resource Guide p. 15 Writer's Handbook p. 25
		____ / 25	18 / 25	

Answer Key

1. D **2. A** **3. C** **4. B** **5. D** **6. C** **7. C** **8. B** **9. D** **10. A** **11. B** **12. A** **13. B**

14. C **15. D** **16. C** **17. A** **18. C** **19. A** **20. B** **21. D** **22. B** **23. C** **24. A** **25. D**

End-of-Year Review

Read the passage. Then read each question. Fill in the correct circle on your answer document.

A Day at the National Zoo

"Good morning, and welcome to the National Zoo," said a young woman in a dark blue shirt as Mr. Pratt's class gathered around. Pointing to the tag on her shirt, she said, "My name is Ramona, and I'll be leading you on your tour today."

"I can't wait to see the monkeys," Connor whispered. "They're my favorite!"

The children followed Ramona as she led them through the zoo. "Our first stop is the elephant house," she said. "Even though we call this area the elephant house, it really houses a few different kinds of animals, including a giraffe, three hippos, and two capybaras, which are large rodents. But the stars of the elephant house are these three elephants."

"Wow!" Leng exclaimed. "They're huge! What's the smallest one's name?"

"The little one is a male elephant named Kandula. He was born here at the zoo a few years ago," Ramona explained. "That's his mother over there. Kandula's birth was especially important because Asian elephants are an <u>endangered</u> species."

"What does that mean?" Tammy asked.

"It means that this kind of elephant might soon become extinct," Ramona replied.

"That means it could disappear forever," Mr. Pratt added. "It is becoming so rare that it may not be around much longer."

"Is there anything people can do to save these animals?" Leng asked.

"That's exactly what we're trying to do," Ramona answered. "The National Zoo houses rare species and gives them a safe place to live. When they have babies, we keep them protected."

"What other protected species live in the zoo?" Myra asked.

"Some of our most famous residents are species that require protection." Ramona said. "For example, we have three giant pandas. The adult male is named Tien Tien, which means 'more and more.' The adult female is Mei Xiang, which means 'beautiful fragrance.' Their baby boy is named Tai Shan, which means 'peaceful mountain.'"

"I remember seeing him on the news!" Kosal exclaimed. "He's really cute."

"He's not as cute as the monkeys," Connor added, causing everyone to laugh. They all knew how much he loved monkeys.

"Actually, we have some very rare monkeys," Ramona said. "If you follow me, I'll introduce you to some golden lion tamarins."

"I thought she said we were going to see some monkeys," Connor groaned. "I don't want to see a lion."

"The golden lion tamarin is a kind of monkey," Ramona explained as the class gathered around the small mammal house. "It got its name because of its puffy orange mane, which makes it look somewhat like a lion. These little monkeys eat fruits, insects, and small lizards. If you look closely at the trees, you'll notice that many of them have small holes in the trunk. That's where the tamarins like to sleep."

Myra pointed to another animal in the small mammal house and asked, "What is that one called? It looks kind of like a raccoon."

"You've got a good eye," Ramona replied. "That's one of our black-footed ferrets, which are also animals in danger of becoming extinct. These small animals have long bodies and usually weigh only one or two pounds. The dark fur around their eyes makes them look like they're wearing a mask. You'll also notice that while they have small legs, they have large paws with claws."

The students watched the animals in the small mammal house until Ramona announced that it was time to move on to the great cats exhibit.

"They have cats at the zoo?" Leng asked. "That seems kind of silly. I see cats all the time around my neighborhood."

"You don't see cats like these," Mr. Pratt replied with a wink.

Ramona turned to face the students and said, "Here we have the great cats, which is what we call lions, tigers, leopards, and other large members of the cat family. Do you see that spotted cat lounging in the grass? That's one of our cheetahs. The cheetah is known for its ability to run very quickly for short distances. It is carnivorous, which means that it eats other animals, such as gazelles and warthogs. Here at the zoo, we feed the cheetahs ground meat."

The class spent the rest of the day moving from exhibit to exhibit, learning about many kinds of animals. At the end of their tour, the students thanked Ramona and then piled back into the bus for the trip back to school. The next day, Mr. Pratt asked the students to write a paper about their favorite animal from the zoo. To no one's surprise, Connor wrote an essay about monkeys.

1. What kind of animal is a capybara?

   A monkey

   B great cat

   C elephant

   D rodent

2. What does the word <u>endangered</u> mean in this passage?

   A a feeling of danger

   B in danger of disappearing

   C in danger of an animal attack

   D free from danger

3. What do the golden lion tamarin and the black-footed ferret have in common?

  A They are both small mammals.
  B They are both large cats.
  C They are both monkeys.
  D They both live in the elephant house.

4. How do you know that this story is told from a third-person point of view?

  A The narrator does not know what is happening in the story.
  B The narrator uses the words *I, we,* and *me.*
  C The narrator tells you what he is thinking.
  D The narrator is not one of the characters in the story.

5. Which of these sentences is most important to the main idea of the passage?

  A *"But the stars of the elephant house are these three elephants."*
  B *"The cheetah is known for its ability to run very quickly for short distances."*
  C *"The National Zoo houses rare species and gives them a safe place to live."*
  D *"It got its name because of its puffy orange mane, which makes it look somewhat like a lion."*

6. How is the information in "A Day at the National Zoo" organized?

  A from least important to most important
  B from most important to least important
  C in sequence
  D from problem to solution

7. What new idea can you form based on the final two paragraphs of the passage?

  A The children got bored as they wandered through the zoo.
  B A cheetah's speed helps it catch prey.
  C All great cats have spots on their bodies.
  D Connor now likes cheetahs better than monkeys.

8. What happens at the beginning of this story?

  A The students write about animals.
  B The students learn about cheetahs.
  C The students learn what problem the zoo is trying to solve.
  D The students visit the small mammal house.

9. Using information in the passage, you can figure out that a *carnivorous* animal is a —

  A meat eater
  B plant eater
  C large animal
  D small animal

10. Read this sentence from the passage.

> "Even though we call this area the elephant house, it really houses a few different kinds of animals, including a giraffe, three hippos, and two capybaras, which are large rodents."

Which of the following words is an antonym of the word *different*?

  A unlike
  B similar
  C strange
  D unknown

Read the passage. Then read each question. Fill in the correct circle on your answer document.

The King of Late Night

John William Carson was born on October 23, 1925, in Norfolk, Nebraska. As a child, Johnny showed an interest in performing in front of a crowd. When he was 14 years old, he created his own magic act and called himself "The Great Carsoni."

When Carson was older, he spent a <u>brief</u> time in college and then joined the navy during World War II. He left the navy in 1946 and went back to school to finish his college education. After graduation, Carson went to work for a radio and television station in Omaha, Nebraska. There, he got his first job as a TV host on an early morning show called *The Squirrel's Nest*. This television program was a springboard to his future.

Carson knew he wanted to make a name for himself in television, so he moved to Los Angeles, California. From 1951 to 1953, he hosted a comedy show called *Carson's Cellar*. A famous comedian named Red Skelton liked the show so much that he hired Carson to come work for him as a writer. One night, Carson stepped in for Skelton and hosted the show. It was a magical moment for him. Carson knew he wanted to be in front of the camera for the rest of his life.

Over the next decade, Carson hosted several shows, but his big opportunity came in October 1962. The NBC television network had a late-night show called *The Tonight Show*. The previous host, Jack Paar, had left the show in March. The show then had a series of guest hosts, but the network was not happy. They wanted a permanent host who would be there night after night. After considering many different performers, they gave Johnny Carson the job.

When he took over *The Tonight Show*, Carson was joined by an announcer and sidekick named Ed McMahon. McMahon sat next to Carson and talked with him before guests came out. He also dressed up to play different parts in short, funny plays called sketches. A few years later, they were joined by a new bandleader, Doc Severinsen, who also joined in on the fun from time to time. He sometimes played a part in sketches and helped Carson with jokes.

Over time, the show established a format that is still used by many television talk shows today. The show started with its theme music playing while McMahon announced who would be on the show. Then he introduced Johnny Carson by saying, "Heeeere's Johnny!" Carson would come out from behind the curtain to greet and talk to the audience. He would stand alone in the middle of the stage and make jokes about what was happening in the news. After that, he would go over to his desk and talk with McMahon for a while before they brought out the first guest.

Carson sat at a desk next to a couch. When a guest came out, the person sitting on the couch would move over so the new guest could be near Carson. By the end of the show, there were often three or four people sitting together on that sofa.

Many different kinds of guests visited the show. There were actors and singers, of course, but Carson also interviewed writers and politicians. Some of his most popular guests were animal handlers and everyday people who had special talents or interesting stories to tell.

As a host, Carson was known for having a quick wit. If something accidentally went wrong on the show or if a joke failed to make people laugh, he would make a funny comment or do a little dance. He made people watching the show forget their troubles as they laughed. Watching Johnny Carson was like taking a short vacation after a long, hard day.

Carson hosted *The Tonight Show* for 30 years. In that time, he helped many performers and comedians find success in show business. His hard work and talent made the show one of the most popular television programs in history. On May 22, 1992, he hosted his last show. Carson had some of his favorite guests on that night, all of whom paid tribute to him.

In his final words to his television audience, Carson talked about how lucky he was for having been able to do something he loved for so long. He thanked Ed McMahon and Doc Severinsen for standing beside him, and then he thanked the viewers for allowing him into their homes night after night. In closing, he said, "I bid you a very heartfelt good night."

After he retired, Carson lived a quiet life. He sometimes appeared as a guest on television programs, and from time to time he wrote jokes and sent them to his friend David Letterman, who had his own late-night talk show. Letterman always used the jokes on his show, which made Carson feel really good.

Johnny Carson died on January 24, 2005, at the age of 79. He will always be remembered as the king of late-night television.

11. Johnny Carson most likely moved to Los Angeles, California, because —

   A there were more television jobs there
   B all his friends lived there
   C he wanted to live a quieter life
   D he didn't like living in Omaha anymore

12. What is the meaning of the word <u>brief</u>?

   A interesting
   B exciting
   C very short
   D very long

13. Which of these sentences best summarizes paragraph 2 of the passage?

   A Carson went to school before and after serving in the navy.
   B During World War II, Carson joined the navy and then went to work on TV.
   C After leaving the navy, Carson finished school and got a job hosting a TV show.
   D Carson's first TV job was hosting a morning show in Omaha, Nebraska.

14. Which of these sentences from the passage includes a metaphor?

A *They wanted a permanent host who would be there night after night.*

B *This television program was a springboard to his future.*

C *As a child, Johnny showed an interest in performing in front of a crowd.*

D *McMahon sat next to Carson and talked with him before guests came out.*

15. What is the main purpose of this passage?

A to describe the life story of Johnny Carson

B to explain the history of *The Tonight Show*

C to help the reader get a job as a television host

D to persuade the reader to watch *The Tonight Show*

16. What does the word *accidentally* mean in the sentence below?

If something accidentally went wrong on the show or if a joke failed to make people laugh, he would make a funny comment or do a little dance.

A in a way that is not accidental

B before an accident

C another accident

D in an accidental way

17. In what way were Johnny Carson and Jack Paar alike?

A Both worked with Ed McMahon.

B Both grew up in Nebraska.

C Both wrote jokes for Red Skelton.

D Both hosted *The Tonight Show.*

18. Which of these sentences from the passage contains an analogy?

A *John William Carson was born on October 23, 1925, in Norfolk, Nebraska.*

B *Watching Johnny Carson was like taking a short vacation after a long, hard day.*

C *Carson had some of his favorite guests on that night, all of whom paid tribute to him.*

D *Letterman always used the jokes on his show, which made Carson feel really good.*

19. Which information from the passage is most important if you are reading to learn why so many people liked Johnny Carson?

A Johnny Carson was friends with David Letterman.

B Johnny Carson was good at making people laugh.

C Johnny Carson hosted several different TV shows.

D Johnny Carson was born and grew up in Nebraska.

20. This passage can best be described as —

A a biography

B a report

C a newspaper article

D an observation log

Read the passage. Then read each question. Fill in the correct circle on your answer document.

Camping Out on Pigeon's Peak

Every month, Linda and Sandy went hiking in the mountains just north of town. It gave them the opportunity to leave their busy lives and get some fresh air.

Though they hiked often, Linda and Sandy knew the mountains could be treacherous for unprepared hikers. A safe trip meant avoiding steep, slippery slopes and being prepared for animal encounters. Most of the time, it was safe to walk along the trails. But during certain parts of the year, hikers had to worry about running into bears. Linda and Sandy weren't worried. They were experienced hikers and always planned their hikes.

On this trip, Linda and Sandy would hike up Pigeon's Peak, camp out, and hike back down the next day. They marked their route on a map so they would always know which trail to take as well as how long it would take to complete the trip. They packed food, clothes, matches, sleeping gear, and a special metal container that they could hang from a tree while they slept. As long as they put their food in that container, animals would not be able to smell it.

When they arrived at the foot of Pigeon's Peak, Linda and Sandy put on their backpacks and began walking up the trail they had picked the night before. It was a bright, sunny day without a cloud in the sky. A light breeze kept Linda and Sandy cool as they climbed. With each step, they admired the lush green vegetation and the animals scurrying along the trail.

Around noon, Linda and Sandy came to a small hikers' station. They signed their names into the logbook and wrote the date and time they had arrived. Many other hikers had also signed the book, noting when they had passed the station on the way up the mountain and on the way back down. Since it was lunchtime, Linda and Sandy sat down and enjoyed some trail mix and beef jerky, shooting the breeze as they ate.

"As we get closer, let's look for a good place to camp for the night," Sandy suggested. "There should be a stream near the peak. We can dip our feet in it."

"Sounds good to me," Linda responded.

After lunch, they finished their hike up the mountain. They took a few pictures at the top and then started back down. Just as Sandy had predicted, there was a small stream near a flat piece of land. Linda and Sandy set up their tent and made a small campfire. Then they unpacked their food and cooked dinner. They were exhausted and fell asleep very quickly.

A short time later, Linda awoke to the sound of low growls outside the tent. She woke Sandy, and the two listened, wondering what was going on.

"Did you remember to lock the food in the special container?" Linda asked.

"I thought you did that!" Sandy whispered back.

They had both forgotten, and now a large bear was poking around their campsite, looking for a midnight snack. When it heard Sandy's voice, the bear stood on its hind legs and growled angrily.

"What are we going to do?" Sandy asked quietly.

"I think we should just stay put," Linda replied. "We'll be safe here."

Just as she spoke, the bear's snout poked through the end of the tent. Its warm breath toasted their toes and they began to panic. Then its paw poked through the flap and brushed their sleeping bags.

Linda screamed and ran out the back of the tent. She wrapped her arms and legs around the trunk of a large tree and quickly climbed to the top. Sandy, on the other hand, could not <u>escape</u>. The bear's paw held her in place. She sat as still as a statue. The mighty beast leaned forward, grunted, and then turned around and went back outside.

Once she was free to move, Sandy reached into her bag and pulled out her emergency whistle. The shrill sound of the whistle frightened the bear, and it quickly ran away. With the bear gone, Linda rushed down to check on her friend.

"Are you all right?" she asked. "What happened?"

Sandy calmly responded, "I'm fine. The bear just wanted to talk, that's all."

"He wanted to talk?" Linda asked, confused. "What did he say?"

Sandy grinned and replied, "When the sun comes up, you two get off my mountain and go home!"

21. Based on information in paragraph 2 of the passage, you can figure out that the word *treacherous* means —

   A very enjoyable
   B very dangerous
   C very humorous
   D very boring

22. In paragraph 4, the writer wants you to imagine that the mountain is —

   A peaceful
   B mysterious
   C crowded
   D dangerous

23. Which information from the passage is least important?

   A Linda and Sandy went hiking up a mountain.
   B A bear came into the tent where Linda and Sandy were sleeping.
   C Linda and Sandy forgot to lock up their food.
   D There was a small stream near Linda and Sandy's campsite.

24. What does the word <u>escape</u> mean in this passage?

   A think of a plan

   B move your body freely

   C get away from danger

   D call someone for help

25. What question might you ask to better understand paragraph 5?

   A Why did all the hikers sign the logbook?

   B What did the trail mix and jerky taste like?

   C How many people signed the logbook before Linda and Sandy?

   D How big was the hikers' station where Linda and Sandy stopped?

26. Which of the following sentences from the passage includes a simile?

   A *Most of the time, it was safe to walk along the trails.*

   B *She sat as still as a statue.*

   C *Linda screamed and ran out the back of the tent.*

   D *The mighty beast leaned forward and licked her face.*

27. Early in the passage, the narrator states that Linda and Sandy are not really worried about bears. This is an example of —

   A hyperbole

   B alliteration

   C flashback

   D foreshadowing

28. Read this sentence from the passage.

> Since it was lunchtime, Linda and Sandy sat down and enjoyed some trail mix and beef jerky, shooting the breeze as they ate.

What were Linda and Sandy doing as they ate?

   A cooking more food

   B looking down quietly

   C having a conversation

   D thinking about dinner

29. The illustration in this passage helps you imagine —

   A why the women were scared of the bear

   B the kinds of food that bears like to eat

   C why the bear stuck its nose in the tent

   D a way to frighten a bear away

30. This passage can best be described as —

   A a letter

   B an observation log

   C a report

   D a story

Read the passage. Then read each question. Fill in the correct circle on your answer document.

Hoover Dam

For many years, people living near the Colorado River faced a problem. Most of the time, the river ran low. But when the snow on the Rocky Mountains melted in the spring, the river flooded. These floods often killed crops and destroyed property. After studying and discussing the problem, the government decided to build a dam.

There were several advantages to building a dam. First of all, a dam would hold back the water in the spring when the flooding began. It would also create a lake that could be used for irrigation, which would allow for more farming. Additionally, turbines could be placed inside the dam. The flowing water would turn them, creating electricity.

One of the strongest supporters of building a dam was the Secretary of Commerce, Herbert Hoover. He worked with people from each of the affected states. Together, they helped figure out ways to distribute the water fairly to each state already getting water from the river. A few years later, Herbert Hoover was elected president.

The project to build the dam was approved in 1928, but that was just the beginning. Not only would this be the biggest dam ever built, but it was also the largest single construction project the government had ever undertaken. It was too big for any one company to handle, so a group of six companies joined together and called themselves Six Companies, Inc. They won the project and put a man named Frank Crowe in charge of building the dam.

Before the dam could be built, Six Companies needed a lot of workers. America was in the middle of the Great Depression, a time when many businesses shut down, putting a lot of people out of work. Six Companies hired so many people that they had to build a town for them to live in. That town was called Boulder City. Workers and their families lived in Boulder City throughout the entire project.

To build the dam, Six Companies also needed dry land to work on. So the first thing the workers were instructed to do was to build two cofferdams in the river around where they planned to build the main dam. Using heavy <u>machinery</u>, the workers dug tunnels through the canyon walls on each side of the river. At first, the river fought against the men. Its flowing water made their work difficult. In the end, though, the workers prevailed. The dams held back the water enough to divert it into the tunnels. When the water reached the other end, the other cofferdam kept the water from flowing back into the work area. This left the area between the two cofferdams dry.

The next step was to remove the loose rock on each side of the canyon where the dam would be built. Men called "high-scalers" wore harnesses with ropes and climbed down the sides of the canyon. Using jackhammers and dynamite, they cleared away the loose rock, leaving a nice solid surface to work with.

The most difficult task the men faced was pouring the concrete. Because the dam was designed to be so large, it was not practical to pour one giant block of concrete. Instead the workers poured it in small sections. They also used a series of pipes filled with river water to help cool the concrete quickly. Without those pipes, it would have taken over 100 years for the concrete to cool completely.

During the construction of Hoover Dam, many new technologies were used. Perhaps the most popular invention was the hard hat. As the workers dug into the sides of the canyon, they were at <u>risk</u> of being injured by falling rocks. To help protect their heads, workers put two baseball caps together and then dipped them in tar. When the tar hardened, it was as solid as steel. These strong hats protected the workers' heads. When the supervisors saw how well the hats worked, they hired a company to produce hard hats made of metal. Today hard hats are used in construction all over the world.

Workers were on the job around the clock. They finished the job in five years—more than two years ahead of schedule. While the dam itself was being built, turbines and power generation equipment were also being constructed. Today Hoover Dam generates power for cities in Arizona, Nevada, and California.

Perhaps the biggest controversy surrounding the dam was its name. When the project was first announced, people started calling it Boulder Dam because it was originally going to be built in Boulder Canyon. However, when the project officially began, the government announced that it would be named after the man who helped start the project, President Herbert Hoover. Many people were upset because they did not like President Hoover. When President Franklin Roosevelt took office, he changed the name back to Boulder Dam. Fourteen years later, however, the name changed again. On April 30, 1947, President Harry S. Truman signed a bill officially restoring the name Hoover Dam.

31. In what way was Hoover Dam different from other dams at the time it was built?

   A It was smaller than any other dam.
   B It was larger than any other dam.
   C It was the only dam made of concrete.
   D It was the first man-made dam.

32. What is Hoover Dam a symbol of?

   A mankind's ability to overcome nature
   B the destructive power of rivers
   C people's belief in the government
   D the danger of digging large tunnels

33. The author mentions the Great Depression in paragraph 5 to help you understand —

   A when the construction of Boulder City was completed

   B why Six Companies decided to build Boulder City

   C how far Boulder City is from Hoover Dam

   D why so many people wanted to work on the dam

34. What does the word <u>machinery</u> mean in this passage?

   A items made with a machine

   B parts of machines

   C large machines

   D like a machine

35. What kind of visual would best show the events that occurred during the construction of Hoover Dam?

   A a photograph

   B a timeline

   C a bar graph

   D an illustration

36. If you want to write a report about Hoover Dam, you should —

   A research facts about the dam

   B create a story about the dam

   C write a letter to the manager of the dam

   D research Herbert Hoover's childhood

37. Which sentence from the passage includes an example of personification?

   A *Its flowing water made their work difficult.*

   B *Workers were on the job around the clock.*

   C *At first, the river fought against the men.*

   D *When the tar hardened, it was as solid as steel.*

38. Which information is most important if you are reading to learn the benefits of Hoover Dam?

   A Construction on Hoover Dam was completed two years early.

   B The dam created a lake that is used for irrigation.

   C Several states get water from the Colorado River.

   D Frank Crowe was in charge of building Hoover Dam.

39. What does the word <u>risk</u> mean in this passage?

   A enjoying your job

   B digging large holes in very hard rock

   C taking a chance that could lead to harm

   D protecting yourself from harm

40. Which of the following words is a homonym for the word *metal*?

   A heavy

   B steel

   C petal

   D medal

Read the passage. Then read each question. Fill in the correct circle on your answer document.

The Anniversary Gift

"Mom and Dad's anniversary is tomorrow," Marissa announced to her younger brother and sister. "What should we get them?"

Each of the kids gathered their savings from their piggy banks. Between them, they had $20.37.

"We've got all the money in the world!" Kara shouted happily. "Let's take Mom and Dad out for a big fancy dinner!"

"We can't do that," Marissa said. "But we could prepare a great dinner for them!"

"We can use the good china and linens," Donald added. "I'll be the waiter, and Marissa can be the cook. Kara can be the hostess, and we'll all clean up together."

When their parents went to work the next day, Donald and Kara started cleaning the house. Marissa walked to the local supermarket and picked out some tasty selections. Using some coupons she found in the newspaper, she was able to get everything they needed without exceeding their budget.

When she returned home, she found Donald vacuuming the carpet and Kara washing the windows. Marissa joined in, and soon the house was sparkling clean.

Next they got to work preparing dinner. Only Marissa was allowed to use the oven, so Donald and Kara helped mix the <u>ingredients</u> and cleaned the dishes. About an hour before their parents were due to arrive home, Donald and Kara set the dining room table for two. After finishing their predinner duties, they washed up and put on their best clothes.

When Mr. and Mrs. Franklin got home that night, they were greeted at the door by Kara, who was wearing a pink dress and had a beautiful ribbon in her hair. She led them into the dining room, where Donald stood in his nicest suit. He pulled out the chair for his mother and handed her a cloth napkin. Then he introduced himself, saying, "My name is Donald, and I'll be your waiter tonight. Your dinner will be ready in just a few minutes."

He went to the kitchen and returned with the food Marissa had prepared. Everything smelled delicious. After serving the food, Donald excused himself to the kitchen. When dinner was over, he came back and cleared their plates. Then all three children came in with a cake they'd baked just for their mom and dad. The children wished their parents a happy anniversary and then sat down to enjoy dessert with them. As they ate, Kara asked, "Did you like your anniversary present?"

"It was perfect," their mom replied.

"This is the best anniversary ever," said their dad.

41. Which sentence best summarizes paragraph 6 of the passage?

   A While their parents are gone, Donald and Kara clean, and Marissa shops.

   B Marissa uses coupons to help save money when she buys groceries.

   C Marissa, Donald, and Kara keep busy while their parents are gone.

   D Marissa, Donald, and Kara wait until their parents leave for the day.

42. Which of the following is a theme of this passage?

   A The best gifts are always expensive.

   B Teamwork helps get the job done right.

   C Never argue with your siblings.

   D Some jobs are best done by yourself.

43. In this story, Marissa is most like —

   A a grocer

   B a waitress

   C a chef

   D a banker

44. What does the word <u>ingredients</u> mean?

   A parts of a mixture

   B things you throw away

   C tools for cooking

   D types of dishes

45. Why are the children in the story making a big dinner?

   A Marissa is very hungry.

   B Their parents are at work and can't make dinner for them.

   C Donald wants to pretend he's a waiter.

   D Their parents are celebrating their anniversary.

46. What is the main problem in this story?

   A The parents forget their anniversary.

   B The parents have to cook a nice dinner.

   C The children want to give their parents an anniversary gift.

   D The children do not know how to cook.

47. Based on the information in the passage, you can figure out that Marissa —

   A does not get along with her siblings

   B is the oldest child in the family

   C works in a local restaurant

   D has trouble managing money

48. Why don't the children take their parents out for a fancy dinner?

   A They don't have enough money.

   B They prefer homemade meals.

   C They can't leave the house.

   D Their parents don't enjoy eating out.

49. Read this sentence from the passage.

   > After finishing their predinner duties, they washed up and put on their best clothes.

   The prefix *pre-* in *predinner* shows that —

   A they did not complete their duties

   B they had many duties to complete

   C they finished their duties after dinner

   D they finished their duties before dinner

50. Which of these sentences from the passage includes an exaggeration?

   A *"What should we get them?"*

   B *"We've got all the money in the world!"*

   C *Everything smelled delicious.*

   D *Next they got to work preparing dinner.*

End-of-Year Review

Extended Response Questions

1. Based on information from "The King of Late Night," how were Ed McMahon and Doc Severinsen alike?

2. Using information from "A Day at the National Zoo," explain how the National Zoo helps protect animals.

....

Writing Prompt

Everyone has had at least one fun adventure with a friend or family member.

Think about a time that you and a friend or family member had a fun adventure.

Now write an essay about this fun adventure.

Hints for responding to the writing prompt:
- Read the prompt carefully.
- Use prewriting strategies to organize your ideas.
- Include details that help explain your main idea.
- Write sentences in different ways.
- Use words that mean exactly what you want to say.
- Look over your essay when you are done and correct any mistakes.

Student _____   Date _____

End-of-Year Review Test Record

Comprehension | Cross out numbers for items answered incorrectly.

Make Connections	3 43	Make Connections:	17 31
Infer	11 47	Compare/Contrast Information	
Ask Questions	25	Ask Questions: Visuals	35
Determine Importance	5 19	Infer: Author's Purpose	15 33
Monitor Understanding	1 48	Determine Importance: Rank Information	23
Synthesize	7	Monitor Understanding: Reflect on Purpose	38 45
Create Images	22	Synthesize: Create a Summary	13 41
Use Fix-Up Strategies	21	Create Images: Use Visuals	29
		Use Fix-Up Strategies: Read On	9

If student has difficulty with Comprehension, use the Comprehension Bridges.

Total Comprehension Score _____ / 24

Target Skills

Identify Point of View	4	Identify Analogies	18
Identify Story Structure	8	Understand Metaphor	14
Understand Simile	26	Understand Personification	37
Understand Symbolism	32	Identify Plot	46
Identify Exaggeration and Hyperbole	50	Identify Foreshadowing and Flashback	27
Identify Theme	42		

If student has difficulty with Target Skills, use the Teacher's Guide lessons.

Total Target Skills Score _____ / 11

Vocabulary

If student has difficulty with Vocabulary, review student's Vocabulary Journal.

2 12 24 34 39 44   **Total Vocabulary Score** _____ / 6

Word Study

Synonyms and Antonyms	10	Idioms	28
Homonyms	40	Suffixes -ly, -fully	16
Prefixes re-, pre-	49		

If student has difficulty with Word Study, use Sourcebook and Teacher's Guide lessons.

Total Word Study Score _____ / 5

Writing: Process Writing

Form: Biography	20	Form: Report	36
Organizational Pattern: Sequence	6	Form: Story	30

If student has difficulty with Writing, use Writing Bridges.

Total Writing: Process Writing Score _____ / 4

Total Score _____ / 50

Answer Key

1. D	6. C	11. A	16. D	21. B	26. B	31. B	36. A	41. A	46. C
2. B	7. B	12. C	17. D	22. A	27. D	32. A	37. C	42. B	47. B
3. A	8. C	13. C	18. B	23. D	28. C	33. D	38. B	43. C	48. A
4. D	9. A	14. B	19. B	24. C	29. A	34. C	39. C	44. A	49. D
5. C	10. B	15. A	20. A	25. A	30. D	35. B	40. D	45. D	50. B

Extended Response Questions

THEME ①   A Call for Freedom

1. What connections can you make between Paul Revere and John Hancock in "On Boston's Freedom Trail"?

2. What connections can you make between Mary Katherine Goddard and Phillis Wheatley in "Women of the Revolution"?

THEME ②   Creating a New Nation

1. Based on information in "The Declaration of Independence," why was Thomas Jefferson upset that Congress edited his words?

2. How did the silversmith and the apprentice in "A Statue Comes Down" know that the sound of the bells ringing meant something important was happening?

How Does Cooking Work?

1. Using information from the essay "Bake Your Own Bread," explain the purpose of yeast in bread dough.

2. Use information from the interview "Let's Get Cooking!" to explain how science is useful in cooking.

THEME **4** What Is Sound?

1. In the story "The Smell of Soup and the Sound of Money—A Tale from Turkey," the traveler does not have any money. How is this information important to the story?

2. Use information from the journal "Sounds Good to Me!" to explain how sound can help you predict where a storm is taking place.

THEME ⑤ Let Freedom Ring

1. Explain why the narrator refers to Harriet Tubman as a conductor in "Harriet Tubman Leads the Way."

2. How did the boys in "A Not Very Well-Kept Secret" know so much about the secret arguments among the delegates writing the Constitution?

THEME ⑥ Balancing Act

1. Based on page 171 of "Being a Judge: An Interview with Julia Packard," how can you tell that Abraham Lincoln was once a judge?

2. What information on page 185 of "Guess Who's Home" helps you figure out that the president is an important world leader?

Ocean Life

1. How does the author of "Squid Attack!" use language to help create images?

2. After reading "Into the Deep," how would you describe the ocean to a friend?

....

THEME **8** Bottom of the Deep Blue Sea

1. Using clues from "The Adventures of Hercules on Sea and Land," explain what the word *superhuman* means.

2. Explain how clues from pages 234 and 235 of "The Mariana Trench" help you figure out what *vents* are.

Exploring the West

1. Explain how the Shaw family's journey in "Thank You, Lewis and Clark!" is different from the journey of Jedediah Strong Smith in "The Life and Travels of Jedediah Smith."

2. Using information from the essay "From Sea to Shining Sea," explain why so many people traveled west in the early 1800s.

· ·

THEME **10** Settling the West

1. Why does the author of "One Hundred Sixty Miles of Bad Weather!" write about the history of the Pony Express before telling Abe's story?

2. Explain the author's main purpose for writing the story "Land Rush!"

THEME 11   What Goes Up Must Come Down

1. How do the illustrations on page 333 of "How Gravity Was Invented" help you better understand the problem the animals face?

2. How do the illustrations on page 344 of "An Out-of-This-World Vacation" help you better understand the process of space travel?

THEME 12   The Science of Sports

1. Based on page 362 of "Famous Firsts," why is Jackie Robinson considered an inspiration to athletes and sports fans?

2. Explain why the information about the curling competition is more important than the information about the sport of curling in "Manny Masters Curling."

THEME 13 — Communication Revolution

1. World Wind is a real computer program available from NASA. Explain why it is important to understand this when reading "Take NASA's World Wind for a Spin."

2. When reading "Cast Your Vote for the Future," why is it important to understand what the Internet is?

THEME 14 — Making Life Easier

1. Write a summary of the story "Hank, Make Your Bed!"

2. Using information from the story "Emilia and the Birthday Party," explain why Emilia decides that she will never put off doing her chores again.

THEME 15 Nature's Building Blocks

1. How does the illustration on page 465 help you visualize where the events in the poem "Five Spring Flowers" take place?

2. Based on the photograph at the top of page 469 of "Amazing Bamboo," explain what it might be like to stand in the middle of a bamboo forest.

THEME 16 Body Systems

1. Using information from "The Tale of Achilles: A Greek Myth," explain why Achilles was considered the greatest hero of the Greek army.

2. Using information from "Smart Food, Smart Choices, Healthy You!" explain how the Food Guide Pyramid can help you stay healthy.

Ongoing Test Practice Answer Key

Theme	S	1	2	3	4	5	6
1	C	D	A	B	B	A	Patrick Henry's speeches urged the colonists to oppose the British king and support the fight for independence.
2	B	A	C	B	A	D	Park probably decided to write about Thomas Paine because Paine was an important figure in the American Revolution who Park did not know much about.
3	D	A	D	C	B	A	John Hancock was the leader of the Second Continental Congress and a key figure in the revolution.
4	A	D	D	C	B	A	Though Aunt Margaret did not win the contest, she was still successful because a cookie company offered to buy her recipe for $1,000.
5	B	B	D	A	B	C	Sound hits the eardrum and causes vibrations. The vibrations travel through the ear and into a fluid, at which point they turn into special messages that travel to the brain.
6	C	B	A	C	D	A	Washington, D.C., was closer to the middle of the country than Philadelphia.
7	A	D	B	A	C	C	Yera feels prepared but nervous as he puts on his fancy suit and tie and places his notes in a brand-new folder.
8	C	D	B	A	C	A	By reading about Cousteau's life and noting that the author calls him an important figure in oceanography, one can determine that *oceanography* means the study of sea life.
9	A	D	A	C	B	B	A sturgeon and plesiosaur are similar in that they both live in water and have large bodies and snouts.
10	B	B	D	A	C	D	The information about John Fremont helps explain how Kit Carson became so popular during his lifetime.
11	C	C	A	D	A	B	Both John Henry and the machine were faster and stronger than most men, but John Henry was able to defeat the machine.
12	A	C	A	B	A	B	Students should list details that support the main idea that the parachute has gone from being an odd idea to a useful invention that has saved many lives.
13	A	A	D	A	C	D	It is important to know Juanita's team has a big game coming up because it helps to explain her family's excitement and why Juanita wants to hit a home run so badly.
14	D	B	C	A	C	D	Scientists created ARPANET so computers could communicate with one another regardless of where they were located.
15	B	D	C	B	A	D	People were amazed when they first saw light powered by electricity.
16	B	C	A	D	B	B	People were not very interested in Mendel's discoveries. Later, when he became an abbot, Mendel was too busy to continue his scientific research.

Extended Response Answer Key

Theme	Question 1	Question 2
1	Paul Revere and John Hancock are American patriots from Boston buried at the Granary Burying Ground.	As writers, Mary Katherine Goddard and Phillis Wheatley played important roles in the Revolutionary War.
2	Thomas Jefferson was upset by the edits Congress made to his words because he felt the changes spoiled his original ideas.	Bells were often rung to communicate a message and/or alarm people. When the silversmith and the apprentice heard the bell, they knew something important was happening.
3	Yeast causes bread to rise and makes it soft and fluffy.	Science is useful in cooking because it explains how heat is transferred.

Extended Response Answer Key (continued)

4	The traveler is unable to buy anything to eat with his bread. When he tries to soak up the smell of the innkeeper's soup, the innkeeper accuses him of stealing.	By counting the seconds between when you see lightning and hear thunder and then dividing that number by five, you can determine a storm's distance in miles.
5	Conductors guided slaves to freedom via the Underground Railroad. Harriet Tubman did the same when she escaped slavery.	The boys worked at the inn where delegates stayed and overheard the delegates' arguments when they brought them food and made their beds.
6	A judge is a person who hears cases. Judge Packard mentions that Abraham Lincoln used to travel on horseback to hear cases.	The president says he negotiates treaties with the powerful leaders of foreign countries, which lets you know he is a powerful world leader.
7	The author uses descriptive language that tells how things feel, look, taste, smell, and sound.	The ocean is mysterious and full of plant and animal life. It becomes colder, darker, and more mysterious the deeper you go.
8	Students should use clues from the passage to explain that *superhuman* means being able to do something beyond what a normal person can do.	Students should explain that clues from the passage help you understand that *vents* are openings through which water can pass.
Mid-Year Review	The Liberty Bell became a symbol of freedom during the American Revolution and antislavery movement. It was given its name in a poem.	Giraffes' long necks, sleep patterns, and unusually large, dark blue tongues make them unique.
9	The Shaw family was vacationing on the river while Jedediah Strong Smith was earning a living as a trapper and trader.	Many people headed west hoping for a better life. To some that meant becoming rich or seeking adventure. To others that meant escaping troubles or having religious freedom.
10	The author gives a brief history of the Pony Express so the reader will understand why Abe rides through the blizzard and why his job is so important.	The author wrote "Land Rush!" to give the reader an idea of what it was like to be a pioneer in 1889 preparing to rush into the Oklahoma Territory to claim free land.
11	Seeing the floating animals with ropes tied around them helps readers realize that without gravity the animals must think of creative ways to keep from floating away.	The illustrations help readers better understand the process of space tourism because they show the various steps of a space launch and return.
12	Jackie Robinson is an inspiration to sports fans and athletes because of his courage and talent. He was the first African American to play baseball in the major leagues, and he won various honors.	The information about the curling competition is more important than the information about the sport of curling because the focus of the story is on Manny's team competing.
13	Knowing World Wind is a real computer program is important because the passage describes the many ways you can use World Wind in your own life.	It is important to understand what the Internet is because the passage asks you to cast your vote for the Internet as the most important invention in communication.
14	Hank wanted to invent a machine to make his bed. He spent a long time working on his invention, but in the end it didn't work.	Emilia will not wait so long to do her chores again because when she tried to do them all at once, she had a few accidents and almost missed the party.
15	The poem's visuals help readers picture the open field where the events in the poem take place.	Readers can imagine feeling small compared to the tall clusters of bamboo trees.
16	Achilles was considered the greatest hero of the Greek army because he could not be defeated in battle.	The Food Guide Pyramid can help you stay healthy if you follow its suggestions for the number of daily servings from each food group.
End-of-Year Review	Ed McMahon and Doc Severinsen both helped Johnny Carson with jokes and sketches on *The Tonight Show.*	The National Zoo aids endangered species by giving them a safe place to live and reproduce so they do not become extinct.

Name _____

Date _____

Theme Progress Test _____

1	Ⓐ	Ⓑ	Ⓒ	Ⓓ
2	Ⓐ	Ⓑ	Ⓒ	Ⓓ
3	Ⓐ	Ⓑ	Ⓒ	Ⓓ
4	Ⓐ	Ⓑ	Ⓒ	Ⓓ
5	Ⓐ	Ⓑ	Ⓒ	Ⓓ
6	Ⓐ	Ⓑ	Ⓒ	Ⓓ
7	Ⓐ	Ⓑ	Ⓒ	Ⓓ
8	Ⓐ	Ⓑ	Ⓒ	Ⓓ
9	Ⓐ	Ⓑ	Ⓒ	Ⓓ
10	Ⓐ	Ⓑ	Ⓒ	Ⓓ
11	Ⓐ	Ⓑ	Ⓒ	Ⓓ
12	Ⓐ	Ⓑ	Ⓒ	Ⓓ
13	Ⓐ	Ⓑ	Ⓒ	Ⓓ
14	Ⓐ	Ⓑ	Ⓒ	Ⓓ
15	Ⓐ	Ⓑ	Ⓒ	Ⓓ
16	Ⓐ	Ⓑ	Ⓒ	Ⓓ
17	Ⓐ	Ⓑ	Ⓒ	Ⓓ
18	Ⓐ	Ⓑ	Ⓒ	Ⓓ
19	Ⓐ	Ⓑ	Ⓒ	Ⓓ
20	Ⓐ	Ⓑ	Ⓒ	Ⓓ
21	Ⓐ	Ⓑ	Ⓒ	Ⓓ
22	Ⓐ	Ⓑ	Ⓒ	Ⓓ
23	Ⓐ	Ⓑ	Ⓒ	Ⓓ
24	Ⓐ	Ⓑ	Ⓒ	Ⓓ
25	Ⓐ	Ⓑ	Ⓒ	Ⓓ

Name _____

Date _____

Theme Progress Test _____

1	Ⓐ	Ⓑ	Ⓒ	Ⓓ
2	Ⓐ	Ⓑ	Ⓒ	Ⓓ
3	Ⓐ	Ⓑ	Ⓒ	Ⓓ
4	Ⓐ	Ⓑ	Ⓒ	Ⓓ
5	Ⓐ	Ⓑ	Ⓒ	Ⓓ
6	Ⓐ	Ⓑ	Ⓒ	Ⓓ
7	Ⓐ	Ⓑ	Ⓒ	Ⓓ
8	Ⓐ	Ⓑ	Ⓒ	Ⓓ
9	Ⓐ	Ⓑ	Ⓒ	Ⓓ
10	Ⓐ	Ⓑ	Ⓒ	Ⓓ
11	Ⓐ	Ⓑ	Ⓒ	Ⓓ
12	Ⓐ	Ⓑ	Ⓒ	Ⓓ
13	Ⓐ	Ⓑ	Ⓒ	Ⓓ
14	Ⓐ	Ⓑ	Ⓒ	Ⓓ
15	Ⓐ	Ⓑ	Ⓒ	Ⓓ
16	Ⓐ	Ⓑ	Ⓒ	Ⓓ
17	Ⓐ	Ⓑ	Ⓒ	Ⓓ
18	Ⓐ	Ⓑ	Ⓒ	Ⓓ
19	Ⓐ	Ⓑ	Ⓒ	Ⓓ
20	Ⓐ	Ⓑ	Ⓒ	Ⓓ
21	Ⓐ	Ⓑ	Ⓒ	Ⓓ
22	Ⓐ	Ⓑ	Ⓒ	Ⓓ
23	Ⓐ	Ⓑ	Ⓒ	Ⓓ
24	Ⓐ	Ⓑ	Ⓒ	Ⓓ
25	Ⓐ	Ⓑ	Ⓒ	Ⓓ

Mid-Year Review

Name _____

Date _____

1	Ⓐ Ⓑ Ⓒ Ⓓ		26	Ⓐ Ⓑ Ⓒ Ⓓ
2	Ⓐ Ⓑ Ⓒ Ⓓ		27	Ⓐ Ⓑ Ⓒ Ⓓ
3	Ⓐ Ⓑ Ⓒ Ⓓ		28	Ⓐ Ⓑ Ⓒ Ⓓ
4	Ⓐ Ⓑ Ⓒ Ⓓ		29	Ⓐ Ⓑ Ⓒ Ⓓ
5	Ⓐ Ⓑ Ⓒ Ⓓ		30	Ⓐ Ⓑ Ⓒ Ⓓ
6	Ⓐ Ⓑ Ⓒ Ⓓ			
7	Ⓐ Ⓑ Ⓒ Ⓓ			
8	Ⓐ Ⓑ Ⓒ Ⓓ			
9	Ⓐ Ⓑ Ⓒ Ⓓ			
10	Ⓐ Ⓑ Ⓒ Ⓓ			
11	Ⓐ Ⓑ Ⓒ Ⓓ			
12	Ⓐ Ⓑ Ⓒ Ⓓ			
13	Ⓐ Ⓑ Ⓒ Ⓓ			
14	Ⓐ Ⓑ Ⓒ Ⓓ			
15	Ⓐ Ⓑ Ⓒ Ⓓ			
16	Ⓐ Ⓑ Ⓒ Ⓓ			
17	Ⓐ Ⓑ Ⓒ Ⓓ			
18	Ⓐ Ⓑ Ⓒ Ⓓ			
19	Ⓐ Ⓑ Ⓒ Ⓓ			
20	Ⓐ Ⓑ Ⓒ Ⓓ			
21	Ⓐ Ⓑ Ⓒ Ⓓ			
22	Ⓐ Ⓑ Ⓒ Ⓓ			
23	Ⓐ Ⓑ Ⓒ Ⓓ			
24	Ⓐ Ⓑ Ⓒ Ⓓ			
25	Ⓐ Ⓑ Ⓒ Ⓓ			

End-of-Year Review

Name _____

Date _____

1	Ⓐ Ⓑ Ⓒ Ⓓ		26	Ⓐ Ⓑ Ⓒ Ⓓ
2	Ⓐ Ⓑ Ⓒ Ⓓ		27	Ⓐ Ⓑ Ⓒ Ⓓ
3	Ⓐ Ⓑ Ⓒ Ⓓ		28	Ⓐ Ⓑ Ⓒ Ⓓ
4	Ⓐ Ⓑ Ⓒ Ⓓ		29	Ⓐ Ⓑ Ⓒ Ⓓ
5	Ⓐ Ⓑ Ⓒ Ⓓ		30	Ⓐ Ⓑ Ⓒ Ⓓ
6	Ⓐ Ⓑ Ⓒ Ⓓ		31	Ⓐ Ⓑ Ⓒ Ⓓ
7	Ⓐ Ⓑ Ⓒ Ⓓ		32	Ⓐ Ⓑ Ⓒ Ⓓ
8	Ⓐ Ⓑ Ⓒ Ⓓ		33	Ⓐ Ⓑ Ⓒ Ⓓ
9	Ⓐ Ⓑ Ⓒ Ⓓ		34	Ⓐ Ⓑ Ⓒ Ⓓ
10	Ⓐ Ⓑ Ⓒ Ⓓ		35	Ⓐ Ⓑ Ⓒ Ⓓ
11	Ⓐ Ⓑ Ⓒ Ⓓ		36	Ⓐ Ⓑ Ⓒ Ⓓ
12	Ⓐ Ⓑ Ⓒ Ⓓ		37	Ⓐ Ⓑ Ⓒ Ⓓ
13	Ⓐ Ⓑ Ⓒ Ⓓ		38	Ⓐ Ⓑ Ⓒ Ⓓ
14	Ⓐ Ⓑ Ⓒ Ⓓ		39	Ⓐ Ⓑ Ⓒ Ⓓ
15	Ⓐ Ⓑ Ⓒ Ⓓ		40	Ⓐ Ⓑ Ⓒ Ⓓ
16	Ⓐ Ⓑ Ⓒ Ⓓ		41	Ⓐ Ⓑ Ⓒ Ⓓ
17	Ⓐ Ⓑ Ⓒ Ⓓ		42	Ⓐ Ⓑ Ⓒ Ⓓ
18	Ⓐ Ⓑ Ⓒ Ⓓ		43	Ⓐ Ⓑ Ⓒ Ⓓ
19	Ⓐ Ⓑ Ⓒ Ⓓ		44	Ⓐ Ⓑ Ⓒ Ⓓ
20	Ⓐ Ⓑ Ⓒ Ⓓ		45	Ⓐ Ⓑ Ⓒ Ⓓ
21	Ⓐ Ⓑ Ⓒ Ⓓ		46	Ⓐ Ⓑ Ⓒ Ⓓ
22	Ⓐ Ⓑ Ⓒ Ⓓ		47	Ⓐ Ⓑ Ⓒ Ⓓ
23	Ⓐ Ⓑ Ⓒ Ⓓ		48	Ⓐ Ⓑ Ⓒ Ⓓ
24	Ⓐ Ⓑ Ⓒ Ⓓ		49	Ⓐ Ⓑ Ⓒ Ⓓ
25	Ⓐ Ⓑ Ⓒ Ⓓ		50	Ⓐ Ⓑ Ⓒ Ⓓ

Writing Checklist

Read the writing prompt. Use the prompt to write a well-organized paper. Use the checklist below to help you improve your writing.

- [ ] I read the prompt carefully.

- [ ] I used prewriting strategies to organize my ideas.

- [ ] I used neat and clear handwriting.

- [ ] I expressed my ideas clearly.

- [ ] I organized my ideas clearly.

- [ ] I supported my ideas with details and examples.

- [ ] I wrote a clear beginning, middle, and end.

- [ ] I used interesting words that mean exactly what I want to say.

- [ ] I wrote different types of sentences.

- [ ] I made sure my writing sounds right and makes sense.

- [ ] I revised confusing parts of my writing to make them clearer.

- [ ] I proofread my writing.

- [ ] I edited for capital letters.

- [ ] I edited for correct punctuation.

- [ ] I edited for correct spelling.

- [ ] I took out unnecessary words and details.

Make sure you have looked at every item in the checklist to make your writing better.